Chameleons

Care and Breeding of Jackson's, Panther, Veiled, and Parson's

---

FROM THE EXPERTS AT
ADVANCED VIVARIUM SYSTEMS™

By Gary Ferguson, Kenneth Kalisch, and Sean McKeown

THE HERPETOCULTURAL LIBRARY™
Advanced Vivarium Systems™
Irvine, California

Karla Austin, *Business Operations Manager*
Nick Clemente, *Special Consultant*
Barbara Kimmel, *Managing Editor*
Kristin Mehus-Roe, *Editor*
Jessica Knott, *Production Supervisor*
Design concept by Michael Vincent Capozzi
Indexed by Melody Englund

Front cover photo by Bill Love. Back cover photo by Paul Freed. The additional photos in this book are by David Northcott, pp. 5, 113, 121, 113; Bill Love, 9, 18, 29, 30, 45, 51, 55, 56, 65, 69, 78, 88, 89, 93, 100, 107, 112, 116, 118, 122, 123, 126, 127; Heather Powers, 11; Zig Leszczynski, 12, 19, 20, 22, 37, 82, 85, 97, 99, 103, 105, 120; Sean McKeown, 15,16; Isabella Francais, 21, 27, 91, 101; Paul Freed, 24, 26, 33, 34, 61, 63, 86, 115, 119, 137; Dennis Sheridan, 38, 103, 127; Gary Ferguson, 41, 43, 48–49 52, 54, 57, 58, 59, 62, 70, 71, 73, 74, 76; Sally Kuyper, 92; John Tashjian, 95; Jim Bridges and Bob Prince, 108; P. Skoog, 129; P. Choo, 131; Kenneth Kalisch, 132, 135

LCCN: 96-183295
ISBN: 1-882770-95-1

An Imprint of BowTie Press®
A Division of BowTie, Inc.
3 Burroughs
Irvine, CA 92618
866-888-5526

Printed and bound in Singapore
10 9 8 7 6 5 4 3 2 1

CONTENTS

INTRODUCTION

Chameleons are primarily an African and Madagascan group of highly specialized, arboreal, insectivorous lizards comprising more than 130 described species. All the Madagascan forms that have been studied are egg-layers, whereas some of the African forms, including the Jackson's chameleon, give birth to live young (Glaw and Vences 1994). For much of the twentieth century, chameleons were placed in their own suborder, Rhiptoglossa; however, taxonomists have recently reclassified chameleons. They are now considered to be related to the agamids and iguanids, and they have been placed into their own subfamily within the family Chamaeleonidae (Glaw and Vences 1994; Zug 1993) and most are in the genus *Chamaeleo*.

Chameleons have been called the masters of camouflage, using various abilities to pass almost unseen through the surrounding environment. They rest motionless or move very slowly and deliberately with a rocking gait so they are not seen by potential predators. Their independently rotating eyes, set like turrets, afford them an unobstructed view of their surroundings in all directions at once, without the need to move their heads or bodies. They are also capable of making their bodies appear more elongated to take on the appearance of a twig or a branch and of laterally flattening their sides to make themselves look like just another leaf on a tree. In addition, these lizards have a highly sophisticated ability to vary their skin pigments to match their surroundings.

The chameleon's ability to change colors has functions other than camouflage. Its normal colors and the intensity of its color signal its moods to other chameleons of the species. As an ectotherm, it can absorb heat from the sun on cool mornings. In the early morning, the chameleon is

A Parson's chameleon (*Calumma parsonii parsonii*), one of the four most popular chameleon species, displays its majestic profile. There are some 130 chameleon species.

usually dark so as to absorb infrared heat. Its colors lighten as its body absorbs more heat and its body temperature rises. Chameleons are renowned for the rapid speed of their skin color change, which occurs through movement of pigment in the skin cells known as chromatophores.

The chameleon's long muscular tongue is a specialized adaptation for arboreal feeding. This lizard can rapidly propel its tongue to as much as one and a half times its body length to capture insect prey. The tip of the tongue is like a moist suction cup that attaches to the prey and rapidly jerks it back into the mouth.

Feet with opposable toes allow the chameleon to grip branches firmly and to move slowly but deliberately between branches to feed or to flee. The long tail is also prehensile. At night, it is curled up while the chameleon sleeps. (If a portion of its tail is lost, the chameleon cannot regenerate it.)

Although chameleons are sometimes considered easy keepers, they have highly specialized needs. While one chameleon species may be appropriate for a relatively inexperienced keeper, others are only for experts. Understanding each species' habitat and natural history can greatly extend chameleons' lives in captivity. The intention of this book is to help new and experienced herpers provide the best care possible for their chameleons.

In this book, we will take a look at the four most commonly kept chameleon species: Jackson's chameleon (*Chamaeleo jacksonii*), panther chameleon (*Furcifer pardalis*), the veiled chameleon (*Chamaeleo calyptratus calyptratus*), and Parson's chameleon (*Calumma parsonii parsonii*). The first three are the most popular and commonly kept because they are the most frequently and easily captive-bred. Captive-bred animals are easier to care for than wild caughts. These four species also have interesting appearances. Jackson's have triceratops horns on their heads, panthers have awesome colors, veileds have an interesting casque on their heads and are very hardy, and Parson's are quite large for chameleons. These species have contributed to the overall popularity of chameleons in captivity.

PART I

Jackson's Chameleon
(*Chamaeleo jacksonii*)

By Sean McKeown

CHAPTER 1

INTRODUCTION AND NATURAL HISTORY

There are three currently recognized subspecies of *Chamaeleo jacksonii*: *C. j. jacksonii*, *C. j. merumontanus*, and *C. j. xantholophus*. Since the original description of the species, there has been considerable confusion about the taxonomy of the subspecies. The Jackson's chameleon (*Chamaeleo jacksonii*) was originally described in 1896 by the Belgium-born curator of the British Museum of Natural History G. A. Boulenger. His initial description was based on a partially grown preserved male specimen that had been donated to the museum by F. J. Jackson. The title of the article describing this initial specimen was "Description of a New Chameleon from Uganda" (Boulenger 1896); however, the actual label on the type specimen clearly indicated that it was collected in the vicinity of Nairobi, in the Kikuyu District of Kenya, in what was

This male lizard's distinctive trio of horns and his sawtooth-shaped dorsal ridge clearly identify it as a Jackson's chameleon, one of the most popular chameleon species.

then part of British East Africa (Eason, Ferguson, and Hebrard 1988). Several years later, in 1903, J. Tornier described what he called *C. j. vauerescecae* from Nairobi. Half a century later, in 1959, the Dutch herpetologist Dirk Hillenius invalidated this subspecies as he found individuals of *C. j. jacksonii* in the general area of their type locality (Nairobi) that clearly fell within the range of Tornier's description (Hillenuis 1959). At about the same time, A. Stanley Rand of the Smithsonian Institution described a smaller form, the Mount Meru Jackson's chameleon, *C. j. merumontana* (Rand 1958). Finally, thirty years later, Perri Eason, Gary W. Ferguson, and James Hebrard undertook field work in East Africa that led to the formal description of a "new" subspecies, a form already well known to herpetoculturists: the Mount Kenya yellow-crested Jackson's chameleon, *C. j. xantholophus*. This significant paper also provided an important overview of variation in *C. jacksonii* (Eason, Ferguson, and Hebrard 1988).

The Jackson's chameleon is a midsize arboreal member of the genus Chamaeleo, indigenous to the neighboring countries of Kenya and Tanzania in East Africa. The nominate form, *C. j. jacksonii*, occurs at areas of midelevation (5,000–8,000 ft [1,520–2,440 m]) in the vicinity of Nairobi, north of the western and southwestern slopes of Mount Kenya and the Aberdare Mountains. It is found at an elevation of 5,000 ft (1,520 m) around Nairobi and at up to 8,000 ft (2,440 m) on Mount Kenya and the Aberdares. Thus far, the Mount Meru Jackson's chameleon (*C. j. merumontana*) has been documented from only the Mount Meru region of Tanzania at mid- and high elevations. The yellow-crested Jackson's chameleon (*C. j. xantholophus*), the most common subspecies in herpetoculture in the United States, is wide ranging at mid- and high elevations on the east and south slope of Mount Kenya (in the country of Kenya) from about 6,000 to 8,000 ft (1,830 to 2,440 m). On the southern slopes of Mount Kenya are areas of intergradation between *C. j. jacksonii* and *C. j. xantholophus*.

The Eason, Ferguson, and Hebrard study found five statistically independent morphological factors in females and

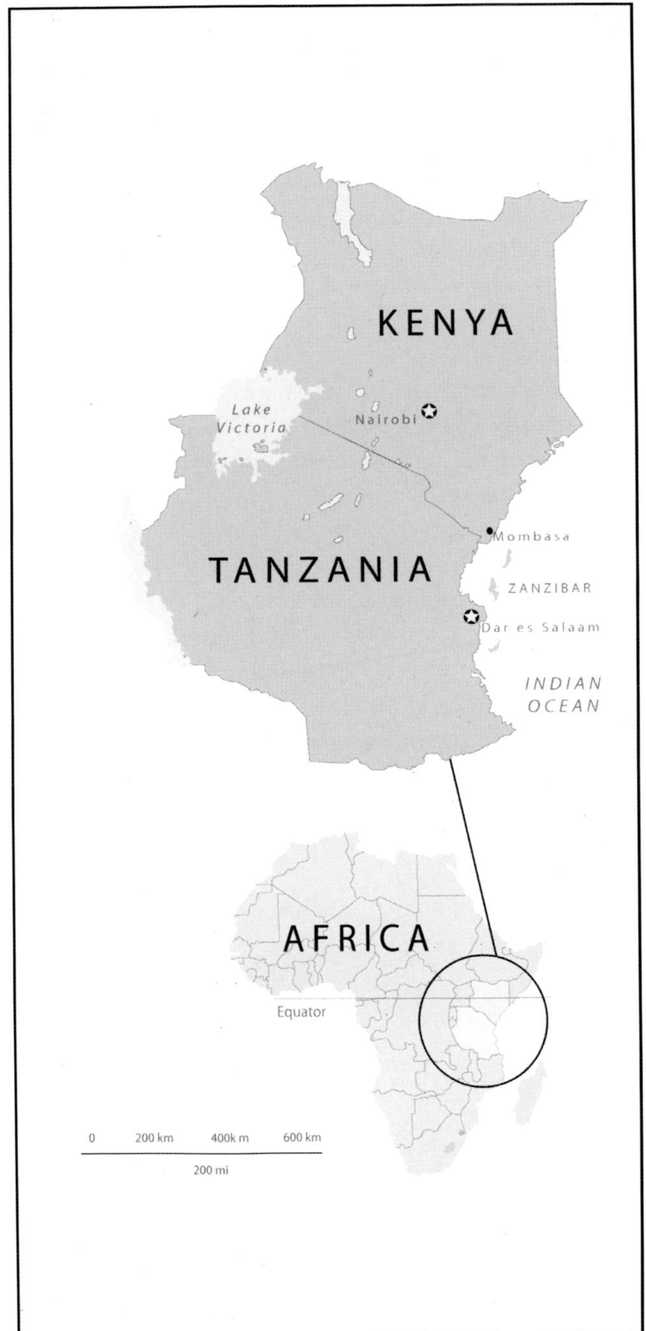

Jackson's chameleons are most commonly found in Kenya and Tanzania in mid- to high elevations where rainfall averages more than fifty inches per year.

four in male Jackson's chameleons that accounted for the variation between known populations of this species. The most important data is summarized in Table 1.

Wild Habitat and Conservation

Jackson's chameleons are most commonly found in Kenya and Tanzania in mid- to high elevations where rainfall averages more than 50 in (127 cm) per year; however, the areas used by these lizards have both wet and dry seasons. Hence, the degree of humidity and the temperature fluctuation depend on the time of the year. Daytime temperatures typically range from 60°F to 80°F (16°C to 27°C), with nighttime temperatures averaging from 40°F to 65°F (4°C to 18°C), depending on the time of year and the specific locality.

With the burgeoning of the human populations in these two African countries during the second half of the twentieth century, large areas of forest have been burned or cleared for agriculture. Fortunately, Jackson's chameleons are generalists and very opportunistic. While they are common in the canopy and edge of primary forested areas, they also have adapted very well to secondary forest and disturbed areas.

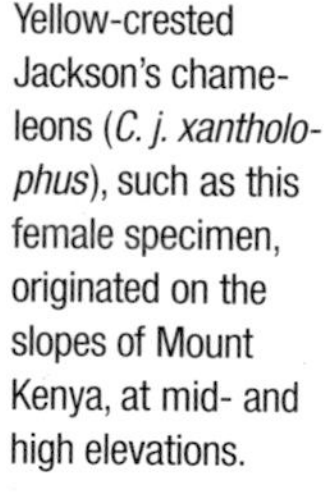

Yellow-crested Jackson's chameleons (*C. j. xantholophus*), such as this female specimen, originated on the slopes of Mount Kenya, at mid- and high elevations.

Table 1: Key to the Three Subspecies of Jackson's Chameleon (*C. jacksonii*)

Diagnostic Variables	*C. j. jacksonii*	*C. j. merumontana*	*C. j. xantholophus*
Snout to vent size (the length of the head and body, not including the tail	4.13 in (105 mm)	3.1 in (79 mm)	4.9 in (124 mm)
Rostral horn in females (the horn at the top of the snout)	Prominent	Prominent	Either absent or greatly reduced in size
Preocular horns in females (the two horns just above and in front of the eyes)	From absent to fully developed	Typically absent	Either absent or greatly reduced in size
Parietal crest pigmentation (color of the ridge at the back of the head)	Dark or dusky	Dusky or light	Light, usually yellow in color
Size of scales at top of parietal crest in males	Raised and rough appearing	Not enlarged and smooth	Not enlarged and smooth
Most characteristic features to distinguish each	Intermediate size; has a greater number of interorbital scales than *C. j. merumontana*	Smaller size and has a lower number of interorbital scales than *C. j. jacksonii*	Largest size; yellow crest

Crops such as coffee, tea, mangoes, and bananas have created increased numbers of insects—including flies, bees, crickets, and grasshoppers—which these lizards readily consume. Population densities of Jackson's chameleons are generally higher in some of the disturbed and agricultural areas than they are in the remaining forests in the national parks (Ferguson, Murphy, and Hudson 1990).

During the early 1960s, Jackson's chameleons were occasionally available in very small numbers from the few reptile importers in the United States. During the late 1960s and the 1970s, when more and more people became interested in reptiles and amphibians, Jackson's chameleons were exported by the thousands each year from Kenya. The primary exporter was Jonathan Leakey, son of the famous anthropologists Louis and Mary Leakey. Most animals Leakey sent overseas were collected for him by local people off the slopes of Mount Kenya. Virtually all the chameleons were the large yellow-crested race, *C. j. xantholophus.* Dealers in America paid three dollars per lizard for the chameleons. They generally retailed in the United States for thirty-five dollars each. Then, in 1981, the Kenyan government totally shut down the trade in Jackson's chameleons. These lizards, which are listed as threatened by the Convention on International Trade in Endangered Species (CITES), were declared a game species. This meant that each lizard would cost many hundreds of dollars for a take permit. No additional Jackson's chameleons legally left Kenya for the United States, Great Britain, Western Europe, or Japan.

Jackson's Chameleons in Hawaii

In 1972, a pet shop owner in Kaneohe on the island of Oahu, Hawaii, was issued a permit by the Hawaii State Department of Agriculture to import one dozen Jackson's chameleons (*C. j. xantholophus*). They were obtained from a large Southern California reptile wholesaler. The lizards quickly sold, and another permit for several dozen was issued. This second group of yellow-crested Jackson's chameleons arrived thin and dehydrated, having been held indoors by the dealer for several weeks after receipt. Thinking that the chameleons could be retrieved as needed, the pet shop owner released the lizards to recover in his well-planted backyard on Kaneohe Bay Drive in Kaneohe, on the windward size of Oahu (McKeown 1978).

Chameleons from this initial population spread through the well-planted mesic (moist) suburban neighborhood. By the late 1970s, populations of Jackson's were established along nearby watershed areas at the base of the Koolau Mountains (McKeown 1978). Today, *C. j. xantholophus* occurs in a number of different geographic areas of Oahu. These lizards continue to expand their range. In fact,

A pair of *C. j. xanthophus* perch on vegetation in Oahu, Hawaii. Introduced to Oahu in the early 1970s, the yellow-crested chameleons can now be found throughout that island as well as on neighboring islands.

between 1984 and the present, virtually every wild-caught Jackson's chameleon for sale in the continental United States has been of Hawaiian origin. Thus, virtually all of the Mount Kenya Jackson's chameleons now bred in the United States mainland have Hawaiian forebears (McKeown 1991).

Jackson's chameleons on Oahu have shown surprising plasticity in adapting to both suburban neighborhoods and low- and midelevation secondary forest, or areas of disturbed vegetation. In addition to natural dispersal, their habit of crossing roadways contributed to their early spread. Upon seeing them walking across a road, motorists often picked them up out of curiosity and later released them in backyards or at other locations. Many hikers took the chameleons home for pets to release in their own yards, or they gave the animals to neighbors for their yards.

Breeding populations of Mount Kenya yellow-crested Jackson's chameleons are now well established in a number of areas on Oahu. Although they are most common to the Koolau Range between Kaneohe and Kailua, large breeding populations exist in many disjunct areas throughout Oahu, even at low elevations on the much drier leeward elevation on the windward side of the island. This species is now also well established at midelevation at several areas on the Kona side of the Big Island of Hawaii and on the island of Maui. These lizards are most common in secondary forest, in disturbed areas, in various types of orchards, and on hedges in residential yards. In upcountry Maui at about 2,500 to 3,000 ft (760 to 910 m) around Makawao, they are so plentiful that it is not unusual to see schoolchildren selling Jackson's chameleons to passing tourists on weekends. The first reports of Jackson's chameleons on Kauai were in 1995.

During the late 1980s and early 1990s, it was illegal to keep Jackson's chameleons in Hawaii according to the Hawaii State Department of Agriculture, which did not want their distribution to increase in the islands. In 1994, after much protest, that ruling was rescinded. As of the time of this writing, Jackson's chameleons are legal to own in Hawaii, but they cannot be taken to other islands or to the mainland.

The interest in these lizards in Hawaii has been phenomenal. During weekends on the main island of Oahu, hundreds of cars are parked along watershed areas while large numbers of people walk through the secondary forest in search of the lizards, which they intend to keep as personal pets or to sell to pet shops. Still other people carry butterfly nets to catch crickets, grasshoppers, large flies, and other insects to feed their pet Jackson's chameleons because commercially raised insects are unavailable in Hawaii. There is so much disturbed and secondary forest area in Hawaii and such an abundant supply of introduced insects that this relatively low-density species surely will continue to expand

A newborn Jackson's chameleon is photographed on Oahu. Jackson's chameleons have become popular pets on the island.

its range in the Hawaiian Islands. The author has closely followed the spread of these lizards there and has as yet seen nothing about them that might be regarded as injurious to Hawaii's specialized endemic invertebrate fauna.

In appearance and size, Hawaiian specimens are much like their Mount Kenya founder stock. The possible exceptions are occasional males with uneven or drooping preocular horns, which may indicate genetic drift. Gary Ferguson has reported, however, that Kenyan specimens sometimes have uneven horns, so variation is seen in African populations as well. Ferguson also believes that horn shape and length may result from a combination of genetics and environment. Under laboratory conditions, high temperatures and improper nutrition produce atypical horn development.

Interestingly, in the Hawaiian Islands Jackson's chameleons are most abundant in areas of moderate rainfall, where daytime temperatures range from 70°F to 90°F (21°C to 32°C) and nighttime temperatures vary from 50°F to 70°F (10°C to 21°C). This temperature range is not too dissimilar from that in their preferred habitats in East Africa, although it is perhaps slightly warmer in some areas.

In addition to the Hawaiian Islands, where large breeding populations occur, tiny populations that appear to be reproductively viable may exist along the coast of California in Morro Bay, Redondo Beach, and San Diego. From time to time, free-ranging individuals turn up in these localities. A Morro Bay population may have originated from a California Department of Fish and Game investigation of a reptile wholesaler living there around 1980. No chameleons were taken, but the agents left open a door to a large outdoor enclosure, and a number of Jackson's chameleons escaped into the surrounding neighborhood.

At irregular intervals, about once a year, a very few of the distinctive Mount Meru Jackson's chameleons (*C. j. merumontana*) have been legally exported from Tanzania to the United States by expatriate importer Joe Beraducci. These infrequent shipments represent the only *C. jacksonii* still coming out from Africa to the United States commercially.

Lifestyle, Behavior, and Arboreal Adaptations

In the wild, Jackson's chameleons live singly. Each individual has its own territory. Virtually all the Jackson's chameleons available in the United States are the larger *C. j. xantholophus* subspecies. An unusually large male can slightly exceed 6 in (15 cm) in head and body length (not including horns) and have a total length slightly more than 12 in (30 cm). A more typical adult male specimen is usually about 5 in (12.7 cm) in snout-to-vent length and 10 in (25.4 cm) in total length. Females usually are slightly more robust but slightly smaller than males.

Generally, birds are the main predators of Jackson's chameleons. In East Africa, several nonvenomous and venomous tree snake species also routinely eat chameleons. If a snake predator approaches, a Jackson's chameleon can flatten its sides, take on dark colors, open its mouth, hiss, and feign biting by rapidly swinging its head around with its mouth wide open. If a predatory bird threatens a Jackson's chameleon, the chameleon can drop from its perching place to the ground and rapidly move to the base of a nearby bush, or it can quickly descend downward into the interior of the bush or tree, where a bird predator cannot follow.

Although female Jackson's chameleons such as this yellow-crested one are usually smaller than male of the species, they are generally more robust.

This *C. j. xantholophus* will use his horns to warn off any potential rival for the attentions of a nearby female.

A male chameleon will defend his territory and defend his right to any nearby female. The horns on a male Jackson's chameleon (and on other chameleon species with preocular and rostral projections) are not merely ornamental. They serve in ritualized combat with other male chameleons of the same species.

For Jackson's chameleons, body size is very important in determining whether combat will occur between two males. Typically, a male will spar only with another male of similar size. If one male is dramatically smaller than another, he will retreat out of the larger male's territory. Initially, a male may rub his horn along the branch he is crawling on as a signal to a relatively nearby male of about equal size that he is ready to engage in ritualized combat. The lizards may approach each other from a horizontal or vertical direction, depending on their positions relative to one another on a tree or a bush. The two males approach quickly and lock horns. Each male uses his horns to push and shove the other. Typically, these territorial battles last several minutes with each individual gaining then losing some ground. Finally, the winner is able to force his opponent to lose his foot grip on the branch (during sparring, the tail is not usually employed to grasp); the loser drops to a lower branch or to the ground. In some contests, one chameleon may be pushed back consistently enough that he chooses to disengage

In Hawaii, two male Jackson's chameleons spar over disputed territory.

and retreat. With little more than his ego deflated, he leaves the immediate area to the winning male. In those situations in which the losing male does not immediately depart, the winning male may pursue, ram, threaten, or attempt to bite until the other lizard moves quickly away.

CHAPTER 2

CAPTIVE CARE

Jackson's chameleons can be obtained directly from breeders and chameleon ranchers at herpetocultural trade shows, ordered from breeders through herpetocultural magazines, and purchased from pet shops. When purchasing a Jackson's chameleon, observe several specimens first and then make the selection yourself. Never purchase any chameleon that appears listless, has sunken eyes, is extremely lightweight, will not feed in front of you, or shows any signs of damage to its mouth or feet. Such an animal will probably not survive for more than a few days. (The normal life span for a captive Jackson's chameleon maintained properly in both indoor and outdoor enclosures is three to eight years.)

The seller should allow you to carefully select the lizard you want. Place your hand in front of and underneath the chameleon so it can crawl onto your hand. Never pull a chameleon off a branch by grabbing it by the body, as you may injure one of its feet or rip off a toenail.

The manner in which a Jackson's chameleon, such as this male yellow-crested, is kept in captivity greatly affects its health and reproductive capabilities.

Once the chameleon is in your hand, gently cup your hand around its body to hold and examine it. The chameleon will not like being restrained in this manner (normally you would only let it crawl on you and not hold it in this way). As a result, it will gape (open its mouth). Look at the inside of the mouth to make sure it does not look infected and the edge is not damaged or dark and crusty. When you return the chameleon to the enclosure, notice whether it uses all four feet and whether both eyes are open and working. Look to be sure the vent opening is not inflamed. The chameleon should appear alert, not listless. There should be no rips or tears on its skin. No signs of runny feces should be present in the enclosure or on the underside of the animal's tail.

Before making a final selection of any lizard, look at it with a magnifying glass. Use the magnifying glass to

This female Jackson chameleon gapes at her photographer, perhaps warning him to keep his distance. If a chameleon gapes at you while you're examining it for possible purchase, look into its mouth to make sure there are no signs of injury or infection.

examine more closely any area of the lizard in question. Be sure as well to look over its entire body with the magnifying glass for signs of mites or other external parasites. If you see mites, pass on every chameleon at that location, and make your selection elsewhere.

How well you make your initial inspection before purchase will probably determine whether your pet will give you a great deal of long-term joy or bring you quick sadness. Sick chameleons generally do not survive, even with good (and expensive) care from a veterinarian.

Initial Steps to Take

First, do not purchase a Jackson's chameleon until you have established a proper environment for it. Ready a large, portable, screened indoor-outdoor enclosure on rollers for your new pet. The minimum size should be 2 ft long × 2 ft wide × 3 ft high (61 cm × 61 cm × 91 cm). You may choose to have separate indoor and outdoor enclosures. Cage furniture should be in place before you bring your chameleon home.

Once your Jackson's chameleon is home, weigh it on a gram scale. The lizard can be placed into a small container to be weighed (be sure to subtract the weight of the container); record the information on a data sheet for each of your chameleons. Weigh your lizards at monthly intervals and any time they look substantially thinner or heavier than normal. Such data can help you determine whether an animal might be gravid (pregnant), is feeding properly, or is ill.

If you work closely with a reptile veterinarian, a fresh stool sample can be placed in a plastic bag and taken to the veterinarian by prearrangement. Be sure that your veterinarian is in and on duty; the sample must be examined when it is fresh. The purpose of a stool sample is to check for various types of worms (internal parasites) that may be present. These can usually be eliminated easily through the use of an appropriate oral parasiticide prescribed by an experienced reptile veterinarian. Finding a veterinarian experienced with reptiles is important; an inexperienced one probably will do you little good.

Husbandry

There are several management regimes suitable for various broad categories of chameleons. The Jackson's chameleon is a midelevation, arboreal, cool-tropical climate, montane species and a generalized feeder. (*Montane* means it lives in the zone of relatively moist cool upland slopes below timberline.) The management recipe outlined will work well for Jackson's and most species of chameleons that fall under this montane category. Remember that they need to be housed individually unless the enclosure is extremely large and well planted. Never house more than one male in an enclosure, no matter how large the enclosure is.

Anyone wishing to keep Jackson's chameleons must plan on having either a large screened enclosure on rollers or one indoor enclosure and one outdoor enclosure for each chameleon or group of chameleons. If you are so fortunate as to live in an ideal climate for Jackson's chameleons, such as Hawaii or a beach city in coastal California, then you need only an outdoor enclosure.

In the captive setting, it's important to try to duplicate the natural environment as closely as possible.

Enclosure

The indoor enclosure must have a vertical format. This is most important because your goal is not to adapt your Jackson's chameleon to a cage but to select or build your enclosure to meet the specific needs of your Jackson's chameleon. Always house individuals singly indoors. The indoor enclosure can be screen (preferable), welded wire

Enclosure Cleanliness

Enclosure cleanliness and good hygiene are critical to success. The enclosure should be clean and fresh smelling at all times. If paper is used for substrate, it needs to be changed about three times weekly. If earth is used for substrate, have a special slotted spoon on hand to remove fecal matter each day.

mesh, or glass. Ideally, the enclosure should be roomy and well ventilated. To avoid abrasions, use plastic rather than wire screening.

Very serviceable screen enclosures can be easily and cheaply built, purchased at reptile trade shows, or ordered through dealers who advertise in herpetocultural magazines such as *Reptiles*. Screened enclosures generally are reasonably priced. They can be readily and quite cheaply obtained in a little larger than minimum size, such as a rectangular enclosure 2 ft long × 2 ft wide × 3 ft high (61 cm × 61 cm × 91 cm). Screened enclosures give the advantage of additional air circulation, which is highly beneficial to a Jackson's chameleon. Ideally, use as large a screened enclosure as you have room for and can afford.

The minimum dimensions for an indoor, Plexiglas, commercially produced, hexagonal enclosure for one chameleon is 21 in in diameter × 19½ in in height (53 × 50 cm). However, the larger the enclosure, the better.

The substrate (material on the enclosure bottom) should be either newspaper cut to the desired shape and size or several inches of good quality topsoil. A potted bush such as a fig (*Ficus benjamina*) should take up most of the inside of the enclosure and should be pruned of small branches that could inhibit the chameleon's movement over the bulk of the small tree.

The Outdoor Enclosure

If you want to keep a Jackson's chameleon, it is your responsibility to have an outdoor enclosure for it. The enclosure can take several forms. If you live in an apartment or a condominium, the enclosure can be placed on your patio or

To thrive, Jackson's chameleons, such as this female *C. j. merumontanus*, must have access to an outdoor enclosure.

porch. If you live in a house, the outdoor enclosure can be built in your yard around a bush that gets morning sun and that affords your chameleon some shade in the afternoon. Ornamental citrus trees make ideal chameleon outdoor habitats over which you can build a hardware wire (heavy screen) cover. Use ¼-inch (6-mm) hardware wire with a wood frame. Install a well-latched and lockable door on one side—large enough to allow you to reach any spot in the enclosure. In extremely warm climates, such as those of Florida, Georgia, and Hawaii, build the enclosure around a bush that gets morning sun only and is shielded from afternoon sun. In the Midwest or the eastern United States, build the enclosure around a bush that gets both morning and afternoon sun. Be sure that the vegetation of the bush is heavy enough to provide sun, shade, and a thermal gradient.

Watering can be as simple as spraying the top of the enclosure with a hose for thirty to sixty seconds twice each day when the weather is sunny or moving a sprinkler to hit a portion of the enclosure. The sprinkler can even be set on a timer. In very warm climates, attach a constant-drip system to the top of the enclosure to help cool the air whenever the temperature rises to 90°F (32°C) or higher. Be sure to use ¼-inch (6-mm) hardware wire rather than plastic screening for the perimeter barrier of the outdoor enclosure to keep out cats, raccoons, opossums, and other potential predators. A latch with a small lock is also useful to discourage the impulse-oriented chameleon rustler.

The frame of an outdoor enclosure may be square, rectangular, or circular. The reason an outdoor enclosure is necessary is that your Jackson's chameleon needs as much outside time as you can give it when the weather is suitable. Jackson's chameleons need to bask using natural sunlight, and they respond extremely well to good airflow. The outdoor time your chameleon gets will help keep it healthy, will allow it to digest its food more effectively, and in human (anthropomorphic) terms, will also help keep its mind and body well toned.

Whenever the air temperature is between 55°F and 89°F (13°C and 32°C), your Jackson's chameleon can be outside during the day. Whenever the daytime temperature is in that range and the nighttime temperature does not drop below 40°F (4°C), your Jackson's chameleon can remain out at night as well. This species of montane lizard thrives on temperature variation. No matter where you live in the United States, there are many days during the warm months when your lizard can be out all the time. There are periods of several hours during the week, even in cooler climates, when it is sunny enough during the late fall, winter, and early spring that your chameleon can go out for portions of the day. In these cool climates, putting your chameleon out a few hours on weekends works well if you are home to monitor weather conditions.

In warm climates, Jackson's chameleons, such as this female, can remain in outdoor enclosures all night.

The best article I have read on the subject of keeping chameleons in captivity was written by Robert Buckley. Buckley points out that all Old World chameleons fare best when maintained in a state of "loose" captivity that allows them to sun themselves, feed, and drink naturally (Buckley 1990). Essentially, the article emphasizes that for a large part of the year, Jackson's chameleons can be housed outdoors in habitat tree enclosures. Buckley's enclosures use an 18-inch-high (46-cm-high) circular plastic barrier around the bottom edge with attached mesh netting. The mesh in the netting must be small enough to prevent chameleons from squeezing through it. This netting over the trees effectively keeps out birds and cats. Special feeding stations and misting systems are also employed. Buckley points out that in addition to saving you money on electric bills, having chameleons living from half to most of the year outside (depending on your climate) exposes them to yearly temperature and photoperiod cycles. Their health and longevity is maintained and enhanced, and their natural reproductive cycles are maximized. The lesson here is to be creative and think big when it comes to outdoor chameleon enclosures.

Lighting, Heating, and Humidity

The top portion of an indoor enclosure should be a screen or welded wire mesh (never glass) and should have a fluorescent light fixture resting on it. Ideally, you should use one ultraviolet (UVA) BL-type black light and one high UVB full-spectrum tube (such as Zoo Med ReptiSun 5.0 or ESU Daylight Bulb). For example, use one ESU Daylight Bulb and one BL-type black light. Generally, these bulbs need to be replaced at six-month intervals to get maximum output. Purchase a timer for the lights, and provide a consistent daily photoperiod of twelve to fourteen hours of light each day.

The ideal temperature is 77°F (25°C) during the day and 62°F (17°C) at night, with a basking spot of 85°F (29° C); however, exact temperatures are not as critical with chameleons as is a suitable temperature range or gradient.

Properly watered plants and earth substrate will help you maintain the correct level of humidity in your chameleon's indoor enclosure.

A suitable daytime indoor range is 75°F–79°F (24°C–25°C), with perching areas (branches) in the enclosure that provide the chameleons with the opportunity to bask under a 40- to 60-watt bulb. Make sure, however, that the chameleon cannot touch the bulb. At another portion of the screen top, place a porcelain-base aluminum reflector hood, and use a 40- to 60-watt incandescent bulb, spotlight, or plant-grow bulb to provide a basking spot for the chameleon.

The nighttime temperature should be in the 60s F (16°C–21°C). If possible, a minimum day-to-night difference of 10 degrees F (5 degrees C) is highly desirable. Do not use hot rocks, heating pads, or heat tapes with these arboreal lizards. A three-prong outlet plug is recommended for use with all electronics and should be plugged into a safety bar (available at any hardware store) for fire prevention.

All chameleons benefit from good airflow. Remember that Jackson's chameleons do not like—and will quickly perish in—hot, stuffy, low-airflow, constant-temperature enclosures.

The live plants and earth substrate should be watered each day to provide moderate, not high, humidity. If the earth substrate is properly watered, the soil should be dry by the next morning. An ideal relative humidity range for Jackson's chameleons is 50 to 75 percent.

Feeding

Jackson's chameleons are insectivorous. They feed on insects and other invertebrates. The food should be an appropriate size for your chameleon, depending on whether it is a juvenile or an adult. Neonates (newborns) will readily eat flightless (vestigial-winged) fruit flies (*Drosophila* sp.) and hatchling to one-week-old (first-stage) crickets. Juvenile and adult chameleons should be offered as much variety in their diet as possible. Crickets are a good base food and should make up at least 50 percent of the diet. Commercially available insects such as wax worms (larvae and adult moths), butter worms, giant mealworms (*Zophobas* sp.), and regular mealworms (*Tenebrio* sp.) should occasionally be supplemented. Most of these insects can be cultured easily at home as well. Right after mealworms shed, they are white in color, and this is the best time to offer them.

Additionally, a sweep net in a vacant field may yield other tasty, relatively soft-bodied insects such as grasshoppers, butterflies, katydids, and cockroaches. These and small garden snails can be fed if they are free of pesticides and snail bait. Netted honey bees can be pinned and their stingers cut off with small scissors. Once the stinger is removed, these devenomized insects will be relished by your chameleon.

Another feeding trick is to place a trimmed piece of meat and fat from your dinner plate near some shrubbery in your backyard during the spring, late summer, or early fall. Flies

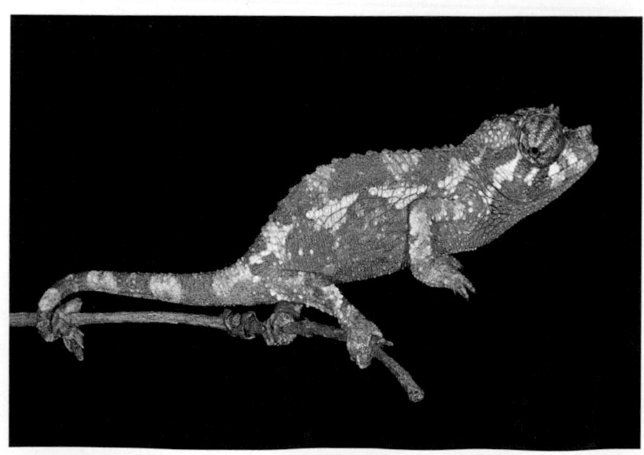

As for an adult, the diet for a juvenile Jackson's chameleon such as this one should be varied, with at least 50 percent of it composed of crickets. Do not overfeed a juvenile by offering adult-size portions.

will gather on the meat. If you quickly place a butterfly net over the meat, the flies will fly to the top of the net. Work one hand up the outside of the net until only a several-inch portion is above your hand. Invert the contents into a clear plastic bag. Tie it off, and place it in the refrigerator. Remember to check the bag at twenty-second intervals. In less than a minute, the flies will be immobilized. They can be dumped onto a piece of newspaper on the table. With a small scissor, cut off the wing on one side only. They are now ready to be emptied into the chameleon enclosure, where they will make a tasty snack for your chameleon.

If your outdoor enclosure is built around a large flowering bush, your chameleon can catch most of its own food during those warmer parts of the year when many insects are present and may need to be fed only supplementally. Observe your chameleon's feeding efforts, weight, and appearance when making such a decision.

An outdoor enclosure on a patio or a porch usually provides the natural, unfiltered sunlight that chameleons need to synthesize vitamin D_3. However, commercially raised insects should be very lightly dusted in a clear plastic bag or plastic jar with a vitamin and mineral powder and a vitamin D_3 source once a week. Shake the container to thoroughly spread the powder on the insects before offering them to the chameleons. Vitamins and supplements for reptiles are available at large pet supply shops, through herpetoculture magazine advertisements, and at reptile trade shows.

It is vitally important that the feeder insects are fed nutritious, balanced diets including alfalfa, whole grain cereal such as uncooked oatmeal, and fresh leafy and yellow or red vegetables so they have a good nutritional balance before being fed to the chameleon. Jackson's chameleons can develop a vitamin A deficiency if not given a good carotene source. Gut-loading is a term used for beefing up purchased crickets for a day or two before they are offered to animals. Professional chameleon breeders also add calcium carbonate or calcium lactate along with multiple vitamins containing vitamin D_3 to the nutritionally balanced cricket diet.

Watering

Most species of chameleons, including Jackson's, have substantial water requirements. Most Jackson's chameleons will not drink from a water bowl; they need simulated rain. You can achieve this either by spraying a fine stream of water at the edge of the mouth of a chameleon using a spray bottle to incite it to drink or using an overhead drip system on a timer. The simplest way to create a drip system is to put water in a suspended plastic (delicatessen) cup with a pinhole in the bottom. Be sure that a similar size or slightly larger receptacle is placed directly underneath it, at the bottom of the enclosure, to collect the water. Do not allow the enclosure bottom to become excessively wet as a result of improper placement of your water-collection container. This will create stuffy, moldy conditions that are unhealthy for your chameleon and can cause respiratory and dermatological problems (Jenkins 1992). Empty the water collection container daily. It is generally best to water the chameleon once and to mist the plants once or twice a day.

Small Children, Dogs, Cats, and Parrots

Wild animals of any sort find it stressful to encounter potential predators and quick movements. Your chameleons should be placed only in quiet, peaceful settings. Their indoor enclosure should be in rooms or other areas that are off limits to all but chameleon-friendly endothermic friends and family members.

CHAPTER 3

REPRODUCTION

One of the greatest joys for a chameleon owner is to breed Jackson's chameleons. The fact that this species is live bearing makes the process much easier because a nesting site for the female is unnecessary and there are no eggs that need to be incubated within a specific temperature and humidity range. Courtship and breeding of the chameleons are best attempted in your outdoor enclosure. Most breeders introduce the female into the male's enclosure. The color of the female's body will indicate when she is ready to mate.

A nonreceptive female will show stress colors and will be mottled with charcoal gray and black shades in her pattern. If approached by the male, a nonreceptive female also may demonstrate aggressiveness, including gaping, hissing, and rocking from side to side; if approached even closer, she sometimes attempts to bite. If you see that the female is nonreceptive, immediately take her back to her own enclosure; try the introductions again at monthly intervals.

Many keepers enjoy the challenge of breeding their chameleons, watching them develop from neonates to juveniles (such as the one pictured here) to adults. Jackson's chameleons are live bearing so breeding them may be easier than breeding other chameleons.

A receptive female usually turns all green or all grayish green and allows the male to approach. He signals his intent by making a series of lateral head-bobbing moves, puffing up, and showing his profile to the female. Male yellow-crested Jackson's (*C. j. xantholophus*) show yellows and blues in their courtship coloration. If the female still appears responsive, the male moves behind the female and mounts her from above. He inserts a hemipenis into her cloacal opening. Actual copulation takes five to thirty minutes. After a successful mating is completed and the two lizards have moved away from each other, the female can be returned to her regular enclosure.

If the female is gravid (pregnant), she will gain weight and take on a very robust appearance over a period of several months. Once it is clear that she is gravid, it is best to house her separately. Before she gives birth, build an inner enclosure liner of nonabrasive plastic screening, and place it inside the hardware wire outer enclosure. The purpose of this is to prevent the neonates from crawling out of the enclosure through the ¼-inch hardware wire barrier. A lost chameleon is rarely recaptured.

The gestation period for Jackson's chameleons is five to ten months, depending partially on the temperatures to which females are exposed. Chameleons are thought to be able to store sperm, a useful technique in some reptiles and one that increases the opportunities to produce offspring among relatively low-density species (Atsatt 1953).

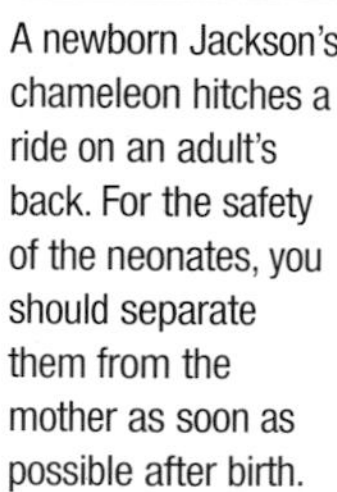

A newborn Jackson's chameleon hitches a ride on an adult's back. For the safety of the neonates, you should separate them from the mother as soon as possible after birth.

While she is gravid, a female may spend more time basking and may increase her food intake until the very last stages of her pregnancy. At this point, she may decrease the number of insects she consumes or even go off feed while continuing to bask, often at several angles. If she is housed primarily indoors, be sure that a basking light is present above the enclosure. From one to several days before the actual birth, the female will become restless and move about throughout the enclosure.

The Birthing Process

The birth process typically takes place in the morning. As the female crawls along the branches, each neonate, or small groups of neonates, drops from her cloaca to the ground below. This process stimulates each neonate to emerge from its own membrane. If a baby does not immediately emerge from the membrane, try gently picking it up and dropping it a second time from the same height to stimulate it to break through its sac. It is possible that several stillborn young or infertile ova (yolks) may be released during the birthing process (DeWitt 1988).

Juveniles and Their Care

The number of young produced by an individual female Jackson's chameleon can be between five and fifty. Generally, older and larger females produce greater numbers of young. The complete birth process may last from thirty minutes to eight hours. In the wild, the young would quickly disperse after being born. To simulate nature as closely as possible, separate the female parent from the newborns as soon as it is clear through your observations that her birthing process is complete. If you leave the neonates in the same enclosure, the female may eat them. The postpartum female should be offered insect food within several hours after she completes the birth process. She will have an extra large appetite for the first couple of weeks after the young are born. Be sure to heavily dust the insects fed to her with a vitamin-mineral powder and vitamin D_3 during this crucial period. Unlike some egg-laying species, female Jackson's chameleons normally survive the birth process if properly managed afterward.

The neonates are a charcoal gray or brown color with off-white striping, barring, and spotting. The only portion of them capable of turning a bright color at this age is the throat area. Should a neonate become stressed, its throat may turn purplish red. Newborn *C. j. xantholophus* typically have three very tiny horns. Neonates have a total length of about 1½ to 1¾ in (38 to 44 mm) and usually weigh about 0.02 ounce (0.6 gram). They are ready to feed within hours of their birth, although initially they are rather clumsy at capturing prey. With practice, they become efficient insect predators.

Some breeders raise juveniles individually on sticks in plastic ice buckets, while others prefer to raise them in small groups in screened enclosures with several plants or bushes to provide climbing cover and individual territory. The young will readily take a variety of invertebrate prey. Vestigial-winged drosophila and hatchling crickets can be cultured as ideal primary food sources. Feed small juvenile chameleons dusted insects daily. Each juvenile will need to consume about six to twelve small insects per daily feeding.

Mist them several times a day. Juveniles can be misted as they are chewing on an insect during feeding, but do not fill the entire mouth cavity with water. This will decrease the chance of a juvenile lizard's accidentally

Handling

No Old World chameleon likes to be excessively handled. Excessive handling may dramatically reduce its life span, although occasional handling is acceptable. Males of this species seem to be more tolerant of handling than the females are. Males that are less shy seem to adjust best to occasional handling. The proper way to handle a Jackson's chameleon is to let it crawl onto your hand. Do not restrain its movements. It may wish to crawl up and rest on your shoulder or nearby on the arm of your chair or couch. When returning it to its enclosure, place your hand under a branch so that it can climb from your hand up onto the branch.

Juvenile Jackson's chameleons, such as this one, can be raised separately or in small groups. Note that juveniles have special feeding and watering requirements.

choking. Do not expose small juveniles to temperature extremes, as their body mass at this age is much less than that of adults. They can overheat and desiccate surprisingly quickly.

The juveniles generally double their size every couple of months. At three to four months of age, more adultlike color-change capabilities and patterns begin to appear, and males begin developing their horns. Coloring capabilities can occur more quickly in males than in females. Adultlike colors in young females may take six to ten months to develop. If you are housing juveniles in groups, be sure to separate any individuals that do not grow as quickly. Young chameleons should be housed only with siblings of similar size, so some mixing and matching will probably be necessary. As the juveniles grow, it's necessary to provide enclosure furniture in the form of appropriate-size live plants. You will also need to offer progressively larger insects.

Conclusion

Jackson's chameleons have specialized captive care requirements. When properly managed, they are relatively long lived and will reproduce in captivity. Proper enclosures and temperature gradients are critical to successful care and breeding.

Acknowledgments

The author wishes to thank Wendy McKeown for her keen observations and insights about Jackson's chameleons in the field in Hawaii and in captivity. The author also extends his appreciation to Gary Ferguson for reviewing the manuscript and to Bob Buckley, Todd Risley, and Cheryl DeWitt for sharing their techniques for managing and breeding Jackson's chameleons in captivity.

As this brightly colored *C. j. xantholophus shows*, Jackson's chameleons are distinctive chameleons that make rewarding and long-lived pets when cared for properly.

PART II

Panther Chameleon (*Furcifer Pardalis*)

By Gary Ferguson, James B. Murphy, Achille Raselimanana, and Jean-Baptiste Ramanamanjato

CHAPTER 4

INTRODUCTION AND NATURAL HISTORY

Like all chameleon species, *Furcifer pardalis* requires a greater attention to detail than do lizards such as leopard geckos. Only hobbyists with a few years of lizard-keeping experience should attempt to keep and breed this species. With proper care, however, its availability, brilliant color, tolerance of warm temperatures, and active but generally nonaggressive temperament make it a fascinating alternative or addition to the other chameleons described in this book.

The panther chameleon is a medium-to-large, highly sexually dimorphic, and often spectacularly colored Malagasy species of chameleon. The species occurs along the coast and on the coastal islands of northern and eastern Madagascar from Ankaramy in the northwest to Tamatave

In Ambanja, Madagascar, a male panther chameleon (*Furcifer pardalis*) blends with his surroundings. Panther chameleons are found along the coast and islands off Madagascar.

on the east-central coast. A locality record for extreme southern Madagascar (Brygoo 1971a) is questionable. A small but viable population, supposedly introduced by humans within historic times, occurs on the remote island of Reunion (310 miles [500 km] east of Madagascar). While males from Reunion resemble those from Nosy Bé (an island off the northwest coast of Madagascar) with overall turquoise coloration, their color pattern is unique in some respects. The species is most abundant at low-elevation coastal localities.

The larger males (up to 22 in [55.9 cm] in total length) vary geographically in color and head ornamentation, while the smaller females (up to 13 in [33 cm]) are more uniform throughout their range (Brygoo 1971a).

Males have a prominent dorsolateral ridge that extends from the back of the head forward over the eye along each side of the dorsolateral border of the snout to the tip or slightly beyond as a small shovel-like projection. The ridge is less prominent in females. Males from some populations (particularly those from the northeastern part of their range) possess a more rounded (as opposed to angular) ridge at the back of the head. There is a low-profiled but well-defined crest on the mid-dorsal line of the back half of the head.

The geographic variation of male color has been described in general terms and has been studied quantitatively by the authors (Ferguson et al. 2004). Adult males from the northwestern insular population (Nosy Bé) tend to be uniformly turquoise or blue-green with spots or patches of red or yellow concentrated on the head and anterior quarter of the torso. The lips are sometimes bright yellow. The degree of facial color is highly variable among individuals, and it increases with age. Although dark vertical bars often appear on the lateral surface of the body and tail when the animal is under stress, these bars are typically faint or absent when in repose.

Males from populations along the coast of Madagascar, from the northwestern town of Ambanja ranging eastward around the northern tip of the island and southward along the northeastern coast to at least the town of Antsiranana (formerly Diego-Suarez), differ subtly from population to

This panther chameleon has the blue coloring common to the adult males of Nosy Bé island. There are a number of color variations found in the panther chameleon, depending on the region of origin.

population, but they share a similar basic color pattern during the breeding season. They possess a green body with some combination of red and blue, usually bold vertical bars. The head, the anterior torso, and sometimes the legs and the tail are commonly brightly colored with red, orange, or yellow. The degree and patterning of this bright coloration is highly variable among individuals and intensifies dramatically during the peak of the breeding season.

During the breeding season, adult males from populations along the east coastal lowlands south from Diego Suarez to Tamatave are dark green to almost black with faint or no vertical bars and a prominent light-colored lateral stripe (males from all populations possess a lateral stripe). This stripe may vary in color or in intensity. Sometimes there is a distinctly lighter dorsal crest. When displaying to a social partner, adult males from these populations rapidly attain a complete suffusion of red or orange or golden yellow over their entire head, body, legs, and tail. Sometimes distinct dark green vertical bars are visible on the flanks, the legs, and the tail. The skin color of the eye turret in all populations is highly metachromatic, changing from a solid color in nondisplay contexts to a pattern of bars radiating from the pupil in social contexts. The color and contrast of these bars is highly variable, both among individuals and among populations.

Adult females from all populations are highly metachromatic, especially when gravid. The basic color of a mature female in a nonsocial context is uniform gray, brown, or faint green with a nondistinct lateral stripe and nondistinct vertical bars. When females are receptive to male courtship, their overall color becomes unpatterned and very pale or sometimes rich orange to pink. When nonreceptive to courtship, they attain a bold pattern of overall dark brown to black with contrasting vertical bars of pink to orange. A bold lateral stripe of the same color is sometimes present. The borders of these bars are very irregular and highly individualized.

The color of juveniles of both sexes is similar among populations. Immature chameleons are uniformly gray or brown with bold darker vertical bars on the flanks. Some become orange or pink at an early stage; when aroused, these juveniles closely resemble a gravid female in color. More typically, aroused or inactive juveniles, especially young hatchlings, become solid dark brown, gray, or black.

The panther chameleon thrives in a warm, humid climate with little seasonal fluctuation in temperature but with dramatic variances in seasonal fluctuation in rainfall. It shuns deeply shaded forest habitat and thrives in forest edge to disturbed agricultural and suburban areas with little natural vegetation. While occasionally climbing to moderate heights of 20 ft (6.1 m) or so, it is very abundant in small shrubs, bushes, and weeds less than 6 ft (1.8 m) in height. In well-developed forest, it may inhabit the crowns of trees (Raxworthy 1988). The grasping power of the feet of the panther chameleon is considerably less than the power of the feet of the related, slightly larger Oustalet's chameleon, with which it is sympatric in the northern part of its range and which can more often be found on thicker, elevated perches (Ferguson et al. 2004).

Despite the abundance of panther chameleons in some areas, breeding males, juveniles, and nonbreeding females are usually well spaced in the habitat. During the breeding season, males and females commonly coexist in close proximity as a pair, but in late summer and fall adult males and females

Panther chameleons, such as this Ambanja male, will bask on cool days to raise their body temperatures to the desired level.

are more often spatially isolated. Introduction of one individual within clear view of another elicits an immediate behavioral response from a resident. Males are fiercely territorial during the breeding season and will inflict severe damage, or death, if allowed to fight. In the late fall season, most adult males are severely scarred, and some are in seriously debilitated condition, possibly from stress from combat.

Panther chameleons seem to prefer warm body temperatures of 85°F–95°F (29°C–35°C) and will bask to attain these temperatures on cool mornings or days. On warm days, they spend most of the daylight hours perched in shade or filtered sun, and their body temperatures match ambient shade temperatures very closely within the above range (Ferguson et al. 2004). Unlike some heliophilic lizards (lizards that bask and generally maintain temperatures higher than the surrounding air temperature), panther chameleons are active on cooler days. In captivity, they seem to adapt well to ambient temperatures in the mid 80sF (29°C–31°C).

Panther chameleons prefer appropriate-size arthropods as food. Although some individuals readily accept small vertebrates in captivity (such as pinkies and small lizards), others do not. They definitely prefer a variety of prey species and will always orient to a palatable new prey item when given a choice (Ferguson et al. 2004). They are voracious feeders, however, and will consume their usual prey item if nothing else is available.

Panther chameleons grow rapidly, reach full size within a year, produce several clutches (each with twelve to fifty eggs) per season, and experience a high annual turnover in nature. Hatching occurs throughout the warm season (September through April) after a six-to-twelve-month egg incubation. Surviving juveniles are sexually mature by the following warm season. Annual survival of mature adults in the field is unknown, but judging by the condition of average to large adult males in May (late fall in the Southern Hemisphere), it is unlikely that many survive to a second season. In addition, considering the high mortality sometimes associated with oviposition (egg laying) in some lizards in the wild (Landwer 1994), annual mortality for females may be very high. Under optimum indoor growing conditions in captivity, hatchlings can reach sexual maturity in less than six months (Ferguson 1994).

The length of the breeding season probably varies geographically. In captivity, Nosy Bé females cycle continuously and produce a clutch of eggs every six to eight weeks. Nosy Bé males appear sexually receptive most of the time, but some have a sexual quiescent (resting) period of one to three months annually. In the field in May, which is late fall in the Southern Hemisphere, juveniles of all sizes are present, and more than 50 percent of the adult females are gravid. These observations suggest a prolonged breeding season. In all other populations, the breeding season appears to be shorter and better defined. In May in Ambanja, Diego-Suarez, and Maroantsetra, small juveniles were not present, and only a small percent of females were gravid. Males from Ambanja and Diego-Suarez have short periods of sexual activity in captivity. A short breeding season has been well documented for panther chameleons on Reunion Island (Bourgat 1970). This is the most southern locality for the species and occurs at the edge of the true southern tropical zone.

CHAPTER 5:

CONSERVATION STATUS

The panther chameleon, like all Old World chameleons, is listed as threatened by CITES. Because of their large size, attractiveness, hardiness, and accessibility, they have become prime targets for exportation by the commercial trade since Madagascar relaxed its restrictions on exporting lizards in the early 1980s. Exportation remained high from 1993 to 2001, with more than 64,000 legally exported between 1971 and 2001 (Carpenter et al. 2004 and 2005). Until the mid-1990s, they were regularly advertised on lists of most of the wholesale reptile dealers in the United States. Currently, only restricted numbers can be exported legally.

Regulations

Without some regulation, commercial exploitation could threaten some populations on a local level. Considering their inability to hide in inaccessible shelters (holes and crevices) and their preference for low perches, it is possible that an entire population can be removed in a short time from a specified area with intensive daytime and nighttime collecting over a few days. A complete removal in early spring before the first oviposition, followed by a complete removal in late fall when most of the previous year's eggs have hatched, could seriously affect—if not eliminate—that local population. However, if collecting is confined to a restricted area or series of small areas within a large, well-dispersed population, these areas would probably be completely restocked by immigration from surrounding habitat within a year. By staggering the exploitation of several such areas, a long-term sustained yield could be maintained indefinitely without harming the ongoing population. Such a strategy has been employed success-

fully by commercial collectors of the green anole (*Anolis carolinensis*) in the southeastern United States.

Although the panther chameleon is basically adapted to disturbed habitat and unlikely to be threatened by forest destruction or moderate collection pressure, some regulation of collection and exportation seems warranted. Restriction of collecting to the mid-to-late breeding season (say, mid-January to mid-February) would allow adults to produce at least one clutch and still be in reasonably robust condition. Although the life expectancy of adults at that time would be only a few months in the field, well-maintained captives treated for

Because it is now considered a threatened species, only limited numbers of panther chameleons can be legally exported from Nosy Bé (shown here) and from elsewhere in Madagascar.

parasites and maintained free of social strife will survive considerably longer (two to five years). Moderate to large juveniles at that time generally undergo considerable density-dependent mortality (mortality that intensifies at higher densities due to many factors associated with crowding and competition for limited resources) as they establish home ranges for the next breeding season. Reducing the density of this age class will increase the survival probability of those remaining or hatching late. Many of those removed, instead of dying in the field, will make robust captives with a high probability of breeding and long-term survival.

Probably the most potentially significant impact of the panther chameleon for chameleon conservation is threefold. First, the panther chameleon is sufficiently appealing and hardy enough to make it an ideal candidate for large-scale managed breeding, both in Madagascar and in first-world consumer countries. Such endeavors would be profitable to commercial herpetologists and would satiate much of the consumer market for captive chameleons in the zoological, educational, research, and private sectors. This, with legislative supervision, could remove much of the exploitation pressure on the more fragile, threatened species, which include most of the fifty-plus chameleon species.

Second, the panther chameleon can serve as a model species to develop and standardize nutrition and husbandry techniques for chameleons in general. While other, more threatened species with different ecological niches are likely to vary in their husbandry requirements, sound knowledge of one or a few species will serve as a good starting point to develop techniques for establishing satellite colonies of species with restricted distributions or from fast-disappearing habitat before they are critically endangered. Projects to study the husbandry of the panther chameleon and other common species are under way (Ferguson et al. 2004).

Third, and perhaps most important, mainstream conservationists have begun to realize the inevitability of widespread degradation of many tropical ecosystems. Even if slash-and-burn agriculture, land development, and human-population growth come to a screeching halt in Madagascar, global warming, in part caused by technology in the developed countries, may be great enough to cause changes in climate that result in significant warming and drying of much of Madagascar's original rain forest (Houghton and Woodwell 1989; Schneider 1989). Forty of Madagascar's fifty-plus chameleon species (the rain forest endemics) may become "naturally" extinct with this climatic change. Madagascar's chameleon fauna may have to diversify all over again. In this scenario, hardy generalized species, which are genetically diverse geographically and can serve as founders for diversification, take on special importance.

Panther chameleons, along with other widespread chameleon species such as *C. oustaleti* and *C. lateralis*, are excellent candidates. Steps should be taken to preserve their diversity, especially in the wild but also in captivity.

Captive Management

Since 1988, the panther chameleon has become readily available in the commercial trade. In June 1992, twelve U.S. zoos reported seventeen males, ten females, and ten juveniles total. This information was compiled by the International Species Inventory System (ISIS). In the August 1992 issue of the *Chameleon Information Network*, forty-five individuals, including many nonprofessionals, reported experience with this species. The breeding potential of a pair of panther

In Ankify, Madagascar, a boy shows off one of the harbor town's panther chameleons. The hardiness of the *Chamaeleo pardalis* has allowed it to adapt to the ever-changing environment in its homeland.

chameleons is enormous. Under ideal conditions, one can expect 30 to 150 viable eggs in a year, depending on the number and size of clutches produced. The incubation plus growth period of the eggs and hatchlings can range from ten to eighteen months. Two and a half years after the initial purchase of a pair, a breeder could conceivably be incubating 450 to 11,250 viable second-generation eggs.

However, the value of the current captive population as a conservation-oriented satellite population is severely limited for several reasons. The major problem is that the locality of origin of imported specimens is largely unrecorded after capture and thus unknown, especially for females. In the past, only a few exporters seemed able to provide locality data, data that would vastly increase the value of the specimens for scientific or conservation projects. Although subspecies are currently not recognized formally, the species do vary greatly geographically in morphology, physiology, behavior, and ecology (Ferguson et al. 2004). Many of the captive-produced hatchlings will be interpopulational hybrids that might be poorly adapted to any current natural habitat in Madagascar. Although the current need for a satellite population to help preserve the species seems small, exporters and importers should realize the importance of providing locality data. Keepers should also realize the importance of keeping good bloodline records for captive-produced hatchlings.

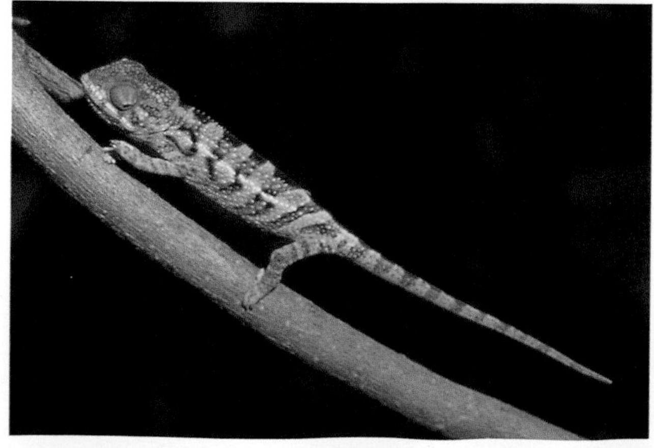

A juvenile panther chameleon makes its way across a slender branch. Captive breeding has become important for the long-term viability of panther chameleon populations.

Another problem with captive management of panther chameleons in the past was variable reproductive success after the first captive generation. While first-generation captive hatchlings maintained exclusively indoors grew, survived, and readily produced eggs in captivity, there often were problems with egg hatchability of these reproductive efforts (Ferguson 1994). The problem was nutritional in origin, relating to dietary vitamins A and D, dietary calcium, and UVB radiation (Ferguson et al. 1996 and 2002)

Total or partial outdoor maintenance is desirable when feasible. The UVB rays from sunlight generate and help regulate vitamin D synthesis. Because fat-soluble vitamins may interact in the body, the sun may help to inhibit the pathological effects of dietary overdose of other fat-soluble vitamins such as A, E, K, and B. This effect of sunlight remains undocumented for any animal, but most keepers believe that animals raised outdoors have fewer developmental and reproductive problems caused by nutrition. Conversely, unpredictable weather changes, predators, escape, and security add risks to outdoor maintenance. Satisfactory artificial sources of UVB are available for indoor maintenance.

Captive management of panther chameleons should begin while the species is still available for exportation. An organized effort should arrange for importation of cohorts from at least six populations accompanied by locality data. A studbook should be established, and specimens should be made available to zoos and qualified nonprofessional chameleon keepers who are willing to participate in the studbook project. The inevitable surplus should be made available to the open market with proceeds returned to support the continuation of the established genetic lines. Provision should be made for outbreeding of each colony. New wild-caught individuals or captive-bred bloodlines should be introduced into a colony every generation or two.

CHAPTER 6

CAPTIVE CARE

In this chapter, we describe some of the husbandry techniques that have proven effective at maintaining panther chameleons in our captive colonies. Panther chameleons are fairly adaptable, however, and other keepers have sometimes used procedures successfully that differ from ours.

Selecting a Chameleon

Panther chameleons can be purchased over the Internet, at some of the larger reptile expos, and sometimes at pet shops specializing in reptiles. When selecting a chameleon to purchase, either wild-caught or captive-born, avoid those that tend to sit with closed eyes or have sunken eye turrets. Avoid chameleons with well-defined vertebrae visible on the back or with noticeable swellings or deformities, especially on the leg joints. If the vent area is soiled, the animal could have a serious gastrointestinal disorder. If possible, observe the animal as it feeds to check for tongue-launching abnormalities.

Although they are very adaptable, panther chameleons, such as this one from Reunion Island, have a number of requirements that must be met when these animals are kept as pets.

A researcher studies a male panther chameleon. Before purchasing a chameleon, always examine it carefully.

Gravid females should be avoided because they will often die soon due to the stress of handling and shipping.

The greatest cause of premature mortality in panther chameleons that are given proper care seems to be parasitic infestation and disease brought in from the wild. A critically important consideration when obtaining recent imports is season. In the Madagascar spring and summer (October through March), adults are actively breeding, undergoing serious territorial disputes, and accumulating high parasite loads. In early spring, robust adults and small juveniles may be obtained. In late spring, adults are still in robust condition, but some treatment for parasites may be necessary if fecal exams reveal their presence. After December, the condition of adults deteriorates until May, when most adults are probably too debilitated to survive long in captivity, even if they survive the rigors of exportation. Only midsize to large juveniles or small adult wild-caught specimens should be obtained after early March.

Healthy adult males obtained in the Malagasy springtime can be expected to survive two to five years in captivity. Females should survive one to two years. Improved knowledge of nutritional requirements might extend captive life expectancies in the future.

Housing

In captivity, panther chameleons seem to adapt to a wide variety of enclosure designs. Enclosures for captive-born adult males ranging from many feet long to those as small as 12 × 12 × 18 in (30.5 × 30.5 × 46 cm) have proven satisfactory. Such small enclosures should be opaque on at least three sides and are recommended only if large numbers of the lizards must be kept in a small area. Despite doing well in most respects, the chameleons may sit on the floor and paw at the sides of small, all-transparent terraria for extended periods. Because panther chameleons (especially some individuals from Nosy Bé) are more active than the

A proper cage is the first item you must provide for your panther chameleon.

Many keepers maintain both an indoor cage, such as the one shown here, and an outdoor cage.

average chameleon, they may not be the best species to keep free-ranging in a tree in a garden room or an enclosed porch. They may drop to the floor or wander into areas where they can cause mischief or injure themselves. Unlike some chameleons, they do not seem to require vegetation for security. In any case, most specimens don't show tendencies to hide in vegetation or to show camouflaging behaviors when approached. Most specimens adapt readily to gentle handling.

If you design a customized enclosure, use a mesh floor with a tray located underneath. This is a standard design for bird and small-mammal enclosures. Feces and dripping water that may overflow from a watering dish resting on the mesh floor will fall to the tray for easy cleaning. Feces will be out of contact range for a chameleon walking on the floor of a cage.

It is critical that any mesh used for chameleon cages be plastic coated or otherwise smooth in texture. Several keepers have reported serious foot and snout damage to

As can be seen in this outdoor cage, panther chameleons do not require a great deal of vegetation inside their enclosures.

chameleons kept in enclosures constructed with standard half-inch hardware cloth or similar rough-textured wire mesh. Even in smooth-mesh enclosures, nose rubbing may occur if the chameleon perceives desirable environmental factors outside the cage (as in the case of a male seeing a female ready to breed). Individuals in mesh cages should be watched closely to prevent this.

The ideal indoor-outdoor enclosures for panther chameleons are standard wire birdcages with plastic bottoms. Ideal mesh size for moderate to large panther chameleons is 1 × ½ inch (2.5 × 1.3 cm) or long wires spaced ½ inch (1.3 cm) apart. Food insects can pass through these enclosures and must be contained in a cup, bowl, or small plastic container. It is essential that enclosures be well ventilated. There must not be glass or transparent plastic on sides exposed to direct sunlight; otherwise, lethally high temperatures may result.

Lighting, Heating, and Humidity

Panther chameleons tolerate diverse light intensity and quality. For aesthetic reasons, the more light, the better. Skylights and insolation of the cage from a window or fluorescent lighting show off the bright colors of the animal better and may actually cause physiological or behavioral enhancement of the animal's color.

Panther chameleons tolerate a wide variety of environments. The most inflexible consideration for their well-being is moderately high environmental temperature. While they can tolerate ranges from less than 48°F (9°C) to more than 100°F (38°C), such extremes are not recommended. Room, cage, and outdoor temperatures should vary from 65°F (18°C) at night to 90°F (32°C) during the day. If maximum environmental temperatures are below 85°F (29°C), a daytime hot spot, preferably a heat-generating light bulb, should be available for basking. If you use an incandescent lightbulb of higher than 25 watts, protect it with a mesh covering to prevent contact burns.

For proper nutrition and successful breeding, UVB exposure is strongly recommended. Indoors, panther chameleons should be provided a gradient of UVB irradiation ranging from zero (full shade) to about 15 microwatts per cm^2 several hours per day. The UVB exposure from a Zoo Med ReptiSun fluorescent bulb at a distance of 1 ft (30.5 cm) will provide an adequate maximum amount.

Panther chameleons, such as this male in Nosy Bé, will do well when exposed to varying degrees of sunlight and fluorescent lighting.

Panther chameleons will voluntarily expose themselves to UVB depending on their internal vitamin D condition (Ferguson et al. 2003). In other words, if they receive high vitamin D in their diet, they tend to avoid exposure to UVB; with low dietary vitamin D, they bask in a high UVB-exposed location. They appear to regulate their exposure better if the UVB and visible light sources are from the same source. Accordingly, some of the newer UVB-emitting nonfluorescent light sources, such as the Westron self-ballasted mercury spot or floodlight or Zoo Med PowerSun bulbs, may be the most desirable. However, they are only for use with larger enclosures (several yards high). Because these bulbs emit considerable heat and UVB, they should be placed so the animal cannot get close enough to overheat (no closer than 3.3 ft [1 meter] for a 160-watt bulb [Gehrmann et al. 2004]). Fluorescent UVB-emitting tubes, such as the Zoo Med ReptiSun 5.0, can be placed closer to the animal (the chameleon can safely come into contact with them) and are more desirable for smaller indoor enclosures. For details on the most effective placement of fluorescent bulbs, consult the articles by Ferguson and others (2002 and 2005) listed in the References.

Despite the high humidity (daytime humidity sometimes exceeds 70 percent on clear summer days) of their habitat, panther chameleons do not seem to require this in captivity. Some keepers report that cage humidity below 35 percent causes shedding problems. We have observed no shedding problems at air humidity of 40 to 50 percent. Regardless of the humidity of the air, to prevent infections it is very important to keep the cage interior, especially perches, completely dry.

Panther chameleons experience variable seasonal climatic fluctuations in the wild. The typical seasons in Madagascar include warmer, wet summers and cooler, dry winters. Within the panther chameleon's range, summer temperatures (day and night averaged) are around 80°F (27°C). Winter temperatures are around 72°F (22°C). These averages differ little throughout the range of the

Although panther chameleons in the wild, such as this male in northern Madagascar, are subject to variable weather conditions, it does not appear necessary to duplicate those cycles in captivity.

species, including Reunion Island. Seasonal rainfall fluctuations vary more across the range of the species. The least seasonal fluctuation in rainfall occurs on Nosy Bé and along the east coast, south of Sambava. The greatest seasonal fluctuation is in the north and northwestern parts of Madagascar, where the natural ecosystem is savannah (grassland with scattered trees and woodlots), and on Reunion Island.

Thus far, first-generation captive panther chameleons seem to breed readily, and those from the more seasonal areas seem to cycle spontaneously without artificial temperatures and moisture cycling. More information on second- and later-generational captives may reveal some need for artificial environmental fluctuations in panther chameleons from certain localities.

Social Management

The best way to maintain panther chameleons is one animal per small- to moderate-size enclosure (dimensions described above). Juveniles can be maintained in small groups if food is available ad libitum and if there is opportunity for visual

A two-month-old panther chameleon and a three-month-old share a perch. Juveniles may be safely maintained in small groups.

isolation provided by vegetation or partial partitioning. Keeping adults in small groups may also work as long as there is only one adult male per group and the most aggressive females are removed. (See further discussion in Chapter 7 under Propagation Techniques.) If hatchlings are initially crowded in small terraria (ten hatchlings per cubic foot [0.03-cubic m]) without the opportunity for visual isolation, they will tolerate such crowding fairly well for several weeks, as long as adequate food is available. However, if hatchlings are isolated for even a short period (one week) and allowed to feed and thermoregulate, their tolerance to subsequent crowding is greatly reduced. Adult males are so territorially aggressive that they will severely injure or kill each other if kept together when in breeding condition, with or without visual isolation opportunities.

Feeding

Although there is considerable knowledge about some elements of nutrition in this and other chameleon species, our greatest ignorance also lies in this area. Many failures of captive management of chameleons by serious herpetoculturists result from our ignorance about proper nutritional balance.

In a laboratory study, food intake of panther chameleons under ad libitum conditions was quantified from hatching to maturity (Ferguson 1991 and 1994). Growing chameleons consume a mass of appropriate-size insects up to an equivalent of their body mass per week. Individuals fed at levels not promoting rapid growth languish and die. Full-size adults of either sex will maintain their body mass and reproduce when eating about thirty to fifty adult crickets per week (about 0.25 to 0.4 ounces [7 to 11.3 grams]).

There are several considerations when presenting food to chameleons. The large numbers of active insects that panther chameleons require should be contained in such a way that they are readily available to the animal without causing it irritation or harm. For example, if ten to twenty crickets are offered to a chameleon in a small plastic terrarium of 3 to 5 gallons (11.4 to 18.9 liters) in volume, the terrarium should contain high perches not touching the floor and a small refuge on the floor for the crickets. The chameleon can retreat to the perch and avoid having crickets crawl over it. In large enclosures, and in those with mesh walls whose mesh spacing is large enough for crickets or other active insects to escape, the insects should be confined in cups at least 6 in (15.2 cm) deep. The sides of the cups should be opaque, so the chameleons will not attempt to feed through the walls, and slick, so the insects will not climb out. Use a curtain pin or similar device attached to the outside rim of the cup and hang it below a favorite perch so the insects can be seen by the chameleon. If you provide crickets to your chameleons ad libitum,

In northwestern Madagascar, a panther chameleon hungrily consumes a cricket.

food and water must also be continually available to the insects. Hungry crickets not only become nutritionally depleted within a twenty-four-hour period but also, unless well contained, will actively seek out and attack the soft tissue of the chameleon while it is sleeping and defenseless. Slices of moist fruit or vegetables, such as apple or potato, and small dishes of nutritionally balanced grain diets will keep crickets well nourished and prevent them from attacking the chameleons.

As we have previously mentioned, a serious gap in our knowledge concerns nutritional quality requirements. Although most herpetoculturists believe crickets, mealworms, and wax worms do not provide a balanced diet for most lizards, opinions vary widely about how much of which nutrient supplements are needed. A major difficulty is that some nutrients—particularly calcium, vitamin A, and vitamin D—are toxic if given in too large a dose. Another serious problem is that nutrient requirements and tolerances may differ among species or even among closely related populations of the same species (L. Talent, pers. comm.). Juveniles, adult males, and adult females, or even individuals within one of these groups, may differ. Well-controlled experiments with carefully manipulated and administered doses and large sample sizes are necessary to increase our understanding of these critical issues. Keeping animals outdoors, where they can receive natural levels of UVB radiation, and feeding them a large variety of wild insect species (not exposed to insecticides or herbicides) is currently the only way to guarantee freedom from nutritional problems. When feeding wild insects, be very careful to use ones that have not been exposed to pesticides or insecticides. Some keepers have reported cases of gout resulting from a diet that includes too many pinkie mice or wax worms.

Powdered vitamin and mineral supplements can be directly applied to insects by dusting them in a plastic bag or cup. Such powders can also be offered on the bottom of feeding containers and will be secondarily picked up by the chameleon's tongue when it feeds. An effective and preferred

This female chameleon from Ambanja requires more calcium and vitamin D_3 than male counterparts do.

alternative involves feeding the supplement to the insect, or gut-loading. The level of supplementation can be more effectively controlled and monitored by this method. Gut-loading also avoids suffocating the insect with the dust and the insect's active attempt to remove the dusted supplement. Crickets, which are voracious omnivores, are excellent subjects for gut-loading (Allen and Oftedal 1989). A nutritionally well-balanced grain diet that includes minerals and vitamin A is the preferred food source for gut-loading crickets. Crickets should have been fed at least twenty-four hours before introducing them to the lizards.

Juveniles and reproducing females seem to require higher doses of calcium and vitamin D_3 than do adult males; however, fortification of cricket food (e.g., grain diet) with calcium in combination with high dietary vitamin D_3 can cause soft-tissue mineralization. This can ultimately prove fatal; thus, low dietary vitamin D_3 concentrations in cricket food in combination with UVB exposure are recommended.

Experiments strongly suggest that endogenous vitamin D_3 produced by exposure to UVB irradiation is necessary for continued health and successful reproduction of panther chameleons. However, while high levels of dietary vitamin D_3 can maintain or restore hatching success (for adult females, 25 IU per week by mouth [L. Talent, pers. comm.]), it may also cause toxemia and shorten the life of a female (Ferguson et al. 1996).

Growing juvenile chameleons seem to require crickets that have eaten cricket food fortified with 50 to 100 IU of vitamin A per gram of cricket food to prevent symptoms such as loss of muscular coordination, spinal and tail kinking and abnormal tail flexure, eye closure, skin lesions, and hemipenal impactions. Keep in mind that the lizard actually gets only a small portion of the vitamin contained in the cricket food. This dose for adult females seems to be the minimum necessary for production of healthy eggs and may be close to deficient. Levels that cause vitamin A overdose symptoms have not yet been determined, but for females direct administration by mouth of 40 IU of vitamin

A in a corn oil solution per week appears to result in healthy hatchlings (L. Talent, pers. comm.). Vitamin A overdose symptoms include gular edema (throat swelling), kidney failure, sterility, metabolic bone disease (caused by bone decalcification), and failure to ovulate in adult females. Vitamin A requirements for panther chameleons may be totally inappropriate for other chameleon species.

In nature, vitamin A is often manufactured by animals themselves from vitamin precursors such as beta-carotene rather than ingested directly in their diet. However, gut-loading crickets with carotenoid-rich vegetables such as carrots, fails to prevent vitamin A deficiency symptoms in chameleons feeding on them. Thus preformed vitamin A is recommended for the panther chameleon.

Watering

A drinking system with water dripping into a small overflow dish that in turn drips through a mesh cage floor will be readily used by the panther chameleon. Most individuals will eventually drink from the dish without water dripping. Suitable drippers include: medical IV drippers, suspended ice cubes that slowly drip water (although some discourage this method because they feel chameleons do not prefer cold dripping water), and suspended rodent drinking bottles heated with a light bulb. Heating causes the air pocket in the bottle to expand and promotes dripping. Some keepers prefer to hand water individuals daily with a pipette or spray bottle, but this is labor intensive if managing a large collection. Juveniles kept indoors in small glass or plastic terraria will readily drink drops from the sides after a light misting.

CHAPTER 7

REPRODUCTION

Breeding chameleons can be interesting and challenging for owners. Before you begin, you need to learn as much as you can about reproduction in panther chameleons and make sure that you have all the necessary equipment—and a compatible mating pair. In this chapter, we will cover sexing techniques, propagation techniques, incubation techniques, egg hatching, and the care of neonates.

Sexing Techniques

Although sexing mature adult panther chameleons is easy based on size, body proportions, and color, sexing immature ones can be tricky. Immature males, especially hatchlings, usually (but not always) have a slightly thicker tail base than do females. Hatchling males have a vestigial pair of hemipenal pockets that almost invariably give the underside of the tail base a more gently tapered profile toward the cloacal aperture. Females sometimes have more orange or pink on the body and more red or orange on the interstitial skin of the gular region, but this is not absolute and can vary geographically. Using these criteria, especially ventral tail-base taper, one can with a little practice sex hatchlings with greater than 90 percent accuracy.

Propagation Techniques

To breed panther chameleons, several setups seem appropriate. Adults can be maintained in isolation, and one individual can be periodically introduced into the enclosure of an opposite-sex individual. If individuals are hand-tamed, merely open the cage door of an individual and hold the other chameleon perched on one's hand in view of the first chameleon. This will elicit a social response

As this Ambanja male panther chameleon (top) and female (bottom) show, males of the species are larger and more dramatically colored than are females.

A female panther chameleon rejects a male by gaping and showing dark colors.

and dictate the next step. It doesn't matter which chameleon is the resident unless the individuals differ in temperament. Then the tamer individual should be the nonresident. Sometimes an isolated male will court too aggressively when first viewing a female. This may elicit a nonreceptive response in a physiologically receptive female. In this case, put the two into visual contact but with actual contact prevented. For example, if a male is in a large display cage, a female can be put into a small plastic terrarium that is placed in the larger enclosure. Usually after a few minutes to a couple of hours, the male will habituate to the female's presence and approach her with more ritualized courtship. Females become receptive to courtship spontaneously upon reaching mature size and within two to three weeks after oviposition. This receptivity is readily apparent by the lightening or brightening of her color and by the subduction of any patterned markings. This display occurs in the absence of her viewing a male. If it persists after she first sees a male, she is ready to mate. The pair can be left together for several days to a couple of weeks, until the female displays nonreceptive color (bold patterning) and behavior (side-to-side rocking with open mouth and lateral compression).

Virgin females will remain in a state of receptivity for up to three months. If the period of waiting has been very long, she will probably assume nonreceptivity immediately or within a few minutes after the first copulation. If placed with a male shortly after becoming sexually receptive (within a few days), she may allow several copulations over a period of several days or a couple of weeks. Nonvirgin females spontaneously assume nonreceptivity after a few days if not given an opportunity to breed. Bred females should be returned to isolation

Usually eggs fertilized from stored sperm are deposited three to six weeks later. Three to six weeks after breeding, females will become increasingly restless, and eggs will become detectable by gentle palpation. At this time, add nesting substrate, consisting of moist (not wet) sand, potting soil, or a combination of the two, 6 to 12 in (15.2 to 30.5 cm) deep to the enclosure. Nesting substrate can be held in a rectangular or cylindrical container placed within her enclosure if space permits.) Alternatively, you can remove the female and place her in an opaque 1- to 5-gal (3.8- to19-L) container filled halfway with nesting substrate. Remove her after two days if she does not begin nest excavation, and reintroduce her in two days. Do not allow

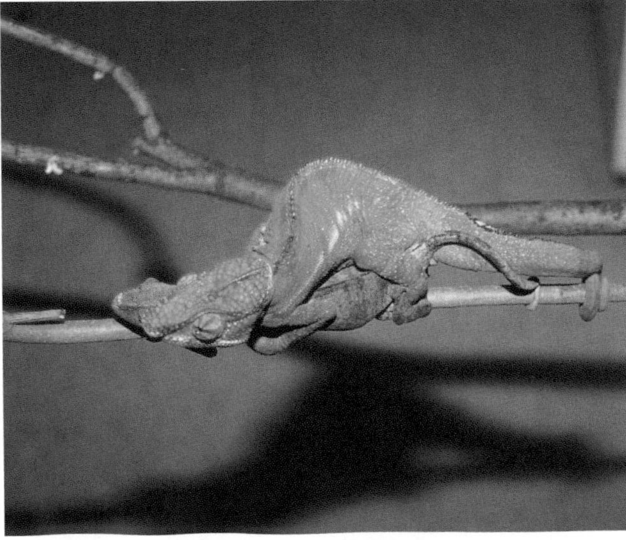

Two panther chameleons from Nosy Bé mate.

insects to roam freely in the container as they may bother her or attack the eggs.

Several keepers have reported a preference by females to dig and nest into the root systems of potted plants. This makes good ecological sense because the open soil in many areas where the species exists becomes extremely dry and brick hard. In such areas, a plant's root systems may be the only place where nests can be constructed and eggs can remain hydrated. Gravid females not given an opportunity to dig a nest will usually oviposit on the floor of the cage, where the eggs will quickly dehydrate and die. Sometimes under these conditions they will retain one to several eggs, which can lead to uterine infections and death; therefore, it is important to keep track of breeding dates and not delay in providing an egg-laying site.

As an alternative to male and female isolation with periodic short-term cohabitation, permanent pairs or breeding groups with one male and up to five females can be maintained. With this method, the cage should be a minimum of 6 ft high × 4 ft long × by 4 ft deep (1.8 × 1.2 × 1.2 m)—the larger the better—sizable enough for individuals to space themselves. Success with groups including multiple females has been mixed. The group should be watched carefully, and aggressively dominant females removed immediately. Individuals raised together since hatching may more likely be compatible. Food and water should be available ad libitum. The onset of nonreceptivity of each female should be noted; females may have to be paint marked for easy recognition by the keeper. Nonreceptive females should be carefully watched for nesting if permanent nesting substrate is available, or if it is not available you should remove restless females as described above. Whether life expectancy is different in such permanent breeding groups has not been verified, but as noted above, breeding males and females are in pairs and seem well spaced in the field when not actively breeding (see also Bourgat 1970). As previously noted, panther chameleons from some populations have well-defined short breeding seasons, while those from other populations breed most of the year. The timing of receptivity and the

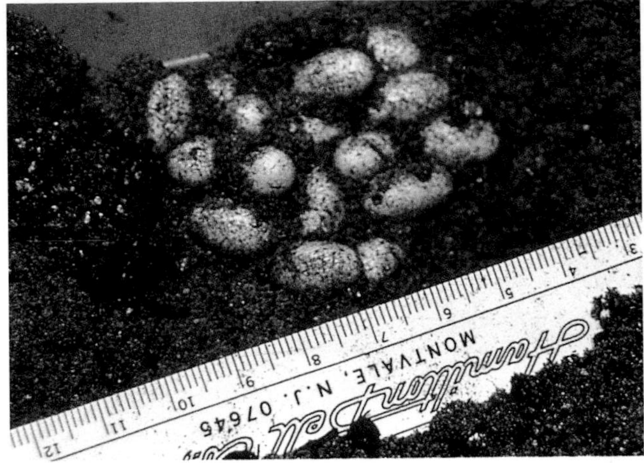

This clutch of *pardalis* eggs has just been excavated. Once oviposited, eggs should be removed and placed in an incubation box.

duration of gestation vary among females but is fairly predictable among cycles of the same female.

Incubation Techniques

After the female has oviposited her eggs in a nest box, the eggs should be removed and placed in an incubation chamber. A female who has recently oviposited will have a noticeably reduced girth and usually have some of the laying substrate clinging to her feet and head. The standard technique for incubating chameleon eggs involves spacing the eggs in a vermiculite-filled container that is sealed or semisealed to hold in moisture. This technique works well for panther chameleons, although it is unnatural. In the field, chameleons construct burrows and lay eggs in a compact mass. The presence of an egg chamber containing an air pocket has not been verified. Indeed, when excavating eggs from a nest box, one gains the impression that an air pocket is absent. Some herpetoculturists have experienced persistent death of chameleon eggs at term (just prior to hatching) with this and other species. Although this is probably a maternal effect related to nutrition or an excess of moisture during late incubation in most cases, the possible need for socially induced hatching cues (such as tactile cues or the moisture of hatching neighbors) has not been ruled out for chameleons.

Panther chameleon eggs may incubate for 180 to 365 days.

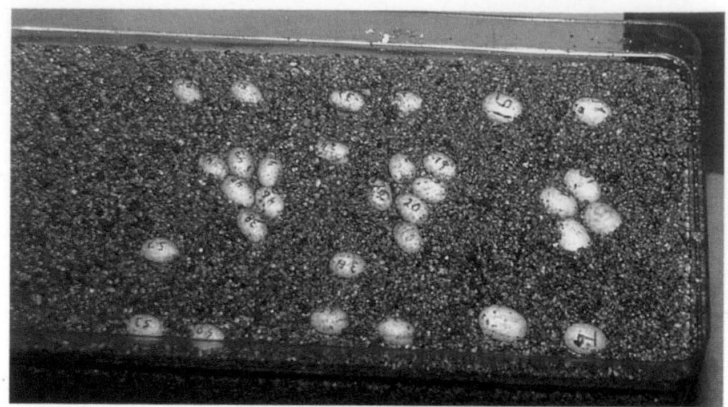

Vermiculite moisture during incubation should average around –400 kilopascals (kPa), which is about 0.7 parts water to 1.0 part dry vermiculite by weight for average grained vermiculite. This should cause the substrate particles to stick together when squeezed but not to drip water. Too much moisture can cause egg bursting and death caused by suffocation of the neonate (baby) at term.

Panther chameleon eggs seem to tolerate a fairly wide range of incubation temperatures. These temperatures influence the duration of incubation, which has been reported to range from 180 to 365 days. Many chameleon species, including the panther chameleon, lay eggs at a very early stage of development. The egg remains at this stage for a defined period of time; that is, it remains in diapause before initiating further development. In captivity, panther chameleon eggs maintained in an incubation medium with a water potential averaging –400 kPa (pressure required for a substrate to take up free water, i.e., slightly moist), and at a day-to-night fluctuating environmental temperature ranging from 65°F to 78°F (18.3°C to 25.6°C), hatch in seven to ten months. The variation seems to be caused by a variable diapause period of three to six months.

The post-diapause initiation of development can be recognized by candling the eggs with strong backlighting. Hold the egg gently between your thumb and a finger, and position the egg between a strong light source and your eye. A yellow transmitted light indicates little embryonic tissue. Pink transmitted light indicates development of blood islets and that dynamic development is in progress. In some Malagasy chameleons, diapause can be prolonged for up to a year if kept at improper temperatures (too high). Infertile or dead eggs spoil rapidly (one week after oviposition or death). Therefore, never discard healthy eggs, no matter how long they have been incubating.

The duration of diapause in the panther chameleon can be influenced by high and low temperatures. A constant incubation temperature of 82°F (28°C) prolongs diapause by two months (Ferguson 1994). A constant incubation temperature of 65°F (18°C) for one or two months followed by a return to the fluctuating temperature range previously cited will break diapause before three months. Because panther chameleon eggs overwinter in Madagascar, cooler winter temperatures may prime eggs still in diapause to initiate development upon the return of warmer springtime temperatures. This might synchronize the hatching of eggs laid at different times, especially if high late summer and fall temperatures prolong diapause.

Eggs are very robust to handling, especially when in diapause. After that they may be handled, but orientation of the egg should not be changed. Newly laid eggs or eggs still in diapause (showing yellow transmitted light) can be shipped without damage as long as extreme temperatures are avoided.

Egg Hatching and Neonates

Healthy neonates generally do not require special treatment at hatching. At term, egg permeability increases, beads of moisture form on the egg surface, and egg dimension decreases noticeably. The neonate slits the eggshell within a few days of these events and usually remains within the eggshell for one or two days while resorbing the external yolk sac. If the shell is not slit by the neonate at this time, the neonate dies. Some herpetologists recommend vigorous spraying of the egg with water or saline solution after the first signs of shell permeability appear. Although this may not be essential for healthy neonates,

Baby panther chameleons can be kept in individual containers such as these.

one should take care to avoid placing the egg in a dry environment between the period of slitting and emergence. To do so may cause shell drying and entrapment of the neonate. If the first few neonates fail to slit the shell and die, one can expect problems with the entire clutch. Vigorous spraying may aid emergence of the strongest individuals. Alternatively, manual slitting of the egg may have the same result.

Neonates will readily adapt to simple small indoor enclosures such as plastic pet habitats, 1-gallon (3.8 liter) jars, 2-gallon (7.6 liter) aquariums, or similar-size outdoor screened enclosures. Enclosures should be free of sub-

Full-spectrum lighting is placed above a row of individual baby panther chameleon enclosures.

strate, contain ample climbing perches, and include small hiding places for crickets. A petri dish or jar lid containing appropriate cricket food should be provided. One to two dozen crickets 1 to 3 mm long should be continuously available. If grain diets are fed to the crickets, the cricket food should be fortified with calcium (1 to 8 percent) and with a vitamin mixture containing preformed vitamin A (50 to 100 IU per gram of cricket food). In addition, UVB irradiation is recommended for juveniles. With a good cricket diet, dusting of crickets is not necessary.

Conclusion

The panther chameleon is a large colorful species that, while more active than some chameleons, has a good disposition and makes an outstanding and attractive pet or exhibit. It is hardy in captivity. Despite an only moderate life span of two to five years, individuals can be bred so successive generational descendants can be maintained over a much longer time span.

Our descriptions of husbandry and reproduction should serve only as guidelines rather than rigid rules. Much of the fun in keeping this animal comes in adjusting the details of husbandry to your own special situation. With careful observation, you can avoid trouble when situations or techniques require adjustment or modification. You must have a local veterinarian experienced in the treatment of reptiles available to handle health problems that may arise.

Acknowledgments

The authors wish to thank Bill Gehrmann, Larry Talent, Steve Hammack, Fred Frye, and Michael Holick for interactions critical to the preparation of this chapter.

As this male specimen from Ambanja shows, the panther chameleon is a large, colorful species that makes for an interesting and rewarding pet.

PART III

VEILED CHAMELEON

(*CHAMAELEO CALYPTRATUS CALYPTRATUS*)

By Kenneth Kalisch

CHAPTER 8

INTRODUCTION AND NATURAL HISTORY

Chamaeleo calyptratus calyptratus is popularly known as the veiled chameleon. It is one of the most widely available and commonly kept chameleons today. The veiled chameleon is a somewhat aggressive, medium to large, spectacularly colored chameleon. It originates in Yemen and parts of the Arabian Peninsula. It is unique among most chameleons in that the males have a high helmet, or casque, on their heads. The females have a smaller version of the cranial casque. Most people who keep chameleons start with this species because of its reputation for being easier to care for than other chameleons. However, *C. c. calyptratus* has been a challenging and often misunderstood chameleon for most hobbyists.

Veiled chameleons have incredible adaptability. They are hardy, tough chameleons, but their adaptability is not without limits. They are just as fragile in their basic needs as any other chameleon. Their care in captivity needs to be taken as seriously as the care of any other species. The veiled chameleon's ability to survive less than ideal circumstances in their natural habitat has led to some of the greatest misconceptions surrounding their care in captivity.

There is an old saying that if you put a chameleon on plaid it will die due to its inability to match the background. This false idea persists today. People familiar with Old World chameleons know the chameleon's coloration is induced by environmental cues such as temperature, lighting, and behavioral indicators. The manifestations of the coloration of a chameleon have nothing to do with what it is

Although somewhat aggressive, spectacular veiled chameleons (*Chamaeleo calyptratus calyptratus*) such as this male are among the most commonly kept of all chameleon species.

sitting on or around. Like their misunderstood coloration changes, there is similar ongoing confusion about the captive husbandry of the veiled chameleon. This chapter provides a basic awareness of captive management and clears up some of the ongoing confusion surrounding the veiled chameleon's care.

Basic Taxonomy

There were originally two forms of veiled chameleon that were formally identified: *C. c. calyptratus* Dumeril and Dumeril, 1851 (Yemen) and *C. c. calcarifer* Peters, 1871 (Asir, Saudi Arabia). The distinguishing feature between them is their casque size. Males and females of both the subspecies have a large cranial casque. The *C. c. calyptratus* subspecies has a higher cranial helmet, while the *C. c. calcarifer* subspecies has a smaller casque height. The male *C. c. calyptratus* casque height can range from 2.7 to 4.3 in (6.9 to 10.9 cm). The male C. *c. calcarifer* casque can reach a height ranging from 1.9 to 2.3 in (4.8 to 5.8 cm). The female casque heights of these two subspecies are smaller than their male counterparts and range from 2 to 2.3 in (5 to 5.8 cm) for *C. c. calyptratus* and from 1.8 to 2 in (4.6 to 5 cm) for *C. c. calcarifer.*

Recent research indicates that *C. c. calcarifer's* classification as a valid subspecies of the veiled chameleon is, with all probability, not valid. Rather, it is believed to be a hybrid from the interbreeding of *C. c. calyptratus* and *C. arabicus*, a similar species that is found within the range of *C. c. calyptratus*. Another similar species found living sympatrically with *C. c. calyptratus* and *C. arabicus* is *C. orientalis*. Additional research must be done to further identify the correct speciation for these chameleons' correct taxonomy.

Male and female *C. c. calyptratus* are sexually dimorphic, that is, they differ in appearance and form. This dimorphism manifests itself in four areas:

- Males typically possess a larger casque height than do females.
- Males have a tarsal spur on each of their hind heels not present in the females.
- Adult males and females display differing coloration.

- Males generally have a greater total body length than do females.

A male *C. c. calyptratus* can reach an adult length of approximately 17 to 24 in (43.2 to 61 cm) from the tip of the snout to the tip of the fully extended tail (tail length ranging from 8.9 to 12.6 in [22.6 to 32 cm]) and a weight of about 3.2 to 6.3 ounces (91 to 179 grams). Female *C. c. calyptratus* can reach a total length of approximately 10 to 13 in (25.4 to 33 cm) (tail length from 5.7 to 7.2 in [14.5 to 18.3 cm]) and a weight of about 3.2 to 4.2 ounces (90 to 119 grams).

The color patterns of *C. c. calyptratus* are highly variable even within the same clutch. Male *C. c. calyptratus* typically have light yellow or gold bands with orange fringes alternating with turquoise to yellow-green bands. The underside and throat areas are typically a light blue-green with dark blue-green spots. Horizontal rows of white patches with dark edges may also be displayed laterally and occur on males and females.

The unique casque of *C. c. calyptratus* may be an important environmental adaptation. It is theorized that it may be used as a method of identification for other chameleons in their area. It may also help them blend into their environment to make them less visible to both predators and prey.

Natural Habitat

On the southern half of the Arabian Peninsula lies southern Saudi Arabia and Yemen, home of *C. c. calyptratus*. This species of chameleon is found in western Yemen and southern Saudi Arabia. It primarily inhabits western Yemen, on the western slopes of a mountain range that starts at Ta'izz and extends north along the west coast of the peninsula through Dhamar, up through Sana'a and into Saudi Arabia. This species is also prevalent on the mountain slopes off the southern tip of the peninsula in south Yemen. A review of documented sightings shows that *C. c. calyptratus* occurs in the rain-fed mountain slopes of southwest and southern Yemen and in the drier central high plateau regions farther

This profile of a young male veiled chameleon shows off the species' most distinguishing feature—its dramatic cranial casque.

north around Dhamar and west of Sana'a (Hillenius and Gasperetti 1984). *C. c. calcarifer* occurs primarily on the drier plains and plateaus along the southwestern coast of Saudi Arabia.

The *C. c. calyptratus* habitat can be divided into roughly three distinct areas: the humid low coastal plains of Yemen and south Saudi Arabia, the rain-fed western and southern mountain slopes of south Yemen, and the high plateaus of north Yemen and southern Saudi Arabia.

Yemen has a narrow coastal plain bordering the Red Sea that continues northward into Saudi Arabia. Here it is extremely humid with average daytime temperatures ranging

This wild veiled chameleon is shown in its homeland of Yemen. The *C. c. calyptratus* come from western Yemen and southern Saudi Arabia.

from 86°F (30°C) in January to 110°F (43°C) in July. Rainfall seldom exceeds 4 in (10 cm) per year. This narrow coastal plain rises steeply to a mountainous interior and in Yemen reaches altitudes above 12,000 ft (3,658 m) near Sana'a. Because of this, moisture evaporated from the Red Sea in the form of clouds hits these mountains and is forced upward to higher altitudes, where the cooler air causes these clouds to condense, forming rain. The southern mountain slopes of Yemen are an exceptional part of the Arabian Peninsula, receiving moderate to abundant rainfall between March and September (nearly half the year). At Ibb, a town just north of Ta'izz, the mountains may receive more than 80 in (203 cm) of rainfall per year. As a result, although most of this area has been cultivated to grow corn, millet, coffee, and dates, semilush vegetation and its associated insect life are seasonally abundant, providing more than adequate conditions for *C. c. calyptratus* to thrive. Average daytime temperatures are milder, ranging from 68°F (20°C) in January to 86°F (30°C) in July, and it is less humid than the low coastal plains. Intermediate between the two extremes of the low coastal plains and rain-fed mountain slopes are the drier high plateaus, which lie around Dhamar just west of Sana'a and farther north into Saudi Arabia. Here there is an almost treeless landscape with no more than 20 in (50.8 cm) of rainfall per year. With the help of irrigation, however, additional crops are grown. In these high plains, severe night frosts can occur. It is theorized that veiled chameleons protect themselves from the frost by climbing down and sleeping in crevices in the ground.

Throughout the mountain slopes and high plateaus, and occasionally down into the low coastal plains, numerous wadis (gullies, or riverbeds that remain dry except during the rainy seasons) channel rainwater runoff from the mountains. Many of these wadis cut deep through the landscape. In some places, these wadis contain water most of the year. Even when they are empty, the moist soil in and around them makes more vegetation possible. Here, it is suspected, lies the key to the ability of *C. c. calyptratus* to survive in the more arid environments. Without vegetation, there would be little insect food available. Correlation of documented sightings with a detailed map of the Arabian Peninsula suggests that veiled chameleons tend to concentrate around the large wadis. Chameleons were sighted in the humid low coastal plain (which receives almost no rainfall) only where a main wadi emptied into the Red Sea. This may explain why one field study documented frequent sightings of *C. c. calyptratus* in areas disrupted by humans, such as cultivated landscapes and even towns, if these changes included an increase in vegetation due to irrigation and landscape maintenance.

The Adaptable Chameleon

Many people believe veiled chameleons are among the easiest chameleons to care for. This is true only to a certain extent. Yes, they are incredibly hardy chameleons. They come from an environment filled with harsh extremes: their natural habitat has sporadic rainfall, inconsistent insect availability, and fluctuating temperatures. To survive the extremes they face in their wild state, they must be adaptable. Yes, they have been able to use this adaptability to survive in captivity. However, this adaptability has encouraged the belief that they aren't as demanding in their captive requirements as other chameleons, which has led to ongoing problems in captivity for the veiled chameleon. Fortunately, these problems can be resolved with proper captive husbandry.

In Yemen, *C. c. calyptratus* lives in a fairly changing and often hostile environment with an inconsistent annual rainfall ranging from 4 to 80 in (10 to 203 cm) per year. The temperatures range from 68°F to 110°F (20°C to 43°C) during the day; nighttime temperatures drop as low as 32°F (0°C). In some of the areas, there is even occasional frost. Veiled chameleons tend to live in wadis or ravines, where there is somewhat more protection and a higher density of foliage and moisture. Their insect food resources are affected by the weather and the seasonal fluctuations.

Veiled chameleons' source of drinking water is also influenced by seasonal availability. Weather reports for some of the areas *C. c. calyptratus* inhabits have recorded no recordable rainfall for as long as three years. The chameleons have adapted to the lack of available water by drinking the morning dew from the morning clouds and ocean mist that collects on the foliage of the plants. Veiled chameleons also receive essential water (and food) through the ingestion of plant matter.

The increase and decrease of food and water combined with the seasonal influences are significant in regard to this species' captive husbandry. The fact that this chameleon has

Contrary to popular perception, veiled chameleons, such as this female, do require careful husbandry to thrive in captivity.

In the veiled chameleon's natural habitat, there are large seasonal variances in food and water availability.

evolved in this extreme and limited environment indicates that it can tolerate a great amount of adversity in its environment. Bring this chameleon into a captive situation, and it seemingly thrives with the abundance it is provided. However, we must expect some change or influence on its long-term outcomes in captivity when we drastically change these parameters.

CHAPTER 9

CAPTIVE CARE

Understanding how this chameleon has adapted to survive its erratic and hostile environment gives us some insight into its needs in captivity. We must translate that knowledge into its captive husbandry.

Purchasing a Veiled Chameleon

The importance of doing research on the species before you purchase your chameleon cannot be emphasized enough. Success with any reptile is based on knowledge of that species. With every new species you work with, you must incorporate a new set of rules. Your overall understanding of a chameleon's requirements will reach a much deeper level through your research. Read everything you can get your hands on. Talk to anyone who currently owns veiled chameleons, join a chameleon Listserv and ask questions there, and buy a book (or several books) on the species. Search the Internet. There are vast amounts of information to be unearthed online. (Remember, however, that not all online writers are equally expert in chameleon husbandry. Take all advice with caution.)

Researching where veiled chameleons occur in the wild and the rainfall and seasonal temperature ranges in these areas will add to your understanding of your pet's requirements. This increased understanding and the small amount of effort it takes to do the research will pay off in the increased success of your chameleon.

Know the breeder you plan to buy from. Understand how he or she cares for the chameleons. To have a strong and healthy adult, it is imperative you start with good stock. Ask sellers what, how much, and how their chameleons are fed, what kinds of supplementation they are given (if any), what type of lighting they are exposed to (natural sun or

Those wishing to own a veiled chameleon should begin by doing research on the species to understand its background and its needs.

artificial, and what types of artificial lights are used), and how they are caged. How your newly purchased baby was raised and how the parents were raised can have long-term effects on your overall success.

A good breeder should be open to giving you the names and phone numbers of previous customers so you can discuss their experiences. Breeders should also commit to helping you with your chameleon if the need arises. All these are good indicators of someone who is committed to doing right in the care of his or her animals.

In Florida, a baby male *Chameleo calyptratus* perches on the plants in its cage. Plants are essential additions to the veiled chameleon's home.

Caging and Furniture

The housing for a chameleon is an area with many choices and much controversy. There are screen, glass, and Plexiglas cages commercially available. Most utilize a combination of these materials. The best choice is a cage made completely of screening. Screening allows for free exchange of airflow, minimizing the risks of potential bacterial growth from too much moisture and allowing the animal to thermoregulate. A screen cage can also be moved outside when weather permits, something not possible with a glass enclosure. Natural sunlight is very beneficial for chameleons.

Chameleons are solitary reptiles so they should be housed separately. The ideal cage should be as large as possible. The minimum cage size for an adult is 24 in long × 24 in wide × 48 in high (61 cm × 61 cm × 122 cm). The top of the cage should be approximately 6 ft (183 cm) from the floor. Some cages are in large free-standing units while other cages must be placed on a table.

The interior of the cage should be well planted with broad-leafed plants such as *Ficus benjamina* or *Schefflera* spp. The plants, in addition to adding to the beauty of the setup, create places for the chameleon to hide in if it feels the need. A word of caution when choosing plants for your chameleon cage: be sure plants are pesticide free and nontoxic.

Chameleons will also utilize perching branches. These should be larger in diameter than the grasp of the chameleon's foot with some variation in size—some branches should be thicker than others. Place the branches at different angles across the cage. Think of the branches as a path for the chameleons to navigate their cage. Be sure to place some branches in the areas intended for basking.

Lighting and Heating

The next step is to provide lighting. Like all chameleons, *C. c. calyptratus* is ectothermic. This species relies on the sun or other forms of heat to regulate its body temperature. Because of the large nighttime temperature drop on the mountain slopes and high plateaus of its native habitat, *C. c. calyptratus* goes through a warm-up cycle each morning, basking intensely in the sun to raise its body temperature to desired levels for activity. The ideal ambient temperature range for *C. c. calyptratus* is 75°F–90°F (24°C–32°C) during the day, with a 10- to 15-degree-Fahrenheit (5- to 8-degree-Celsius) drop at night. Use a basking lighting to allow for thermoregulation.

The two most common and easily accessible forms of heat and light are incandescent and fluorescent UVB lights. Used together, they will provide the basic light and heat within the cage. The fluorescent light is the main source of overall light, with the incandescent providing a basking heat source for the chameleon to use for thermoregulation. Place the fluorescent fixture several inches above the top of the cage, and place the basking incandescent light several inches

In the wild, veiled chameleons can thermoregulate with sunlight. In captivity, they need a basking light.

farther away. Heat-loving *C. c. calyptratus* specimens have been observed basking under basking lights even with the ambient temperatures at 80°F–90°F (27°C–32°C). In captivity, take care to assure that the basking lights are placed at a safe distance to prevent thermal burns from the lighting. Fluorescent lights should be 2 to 4 in (5 to 10 cm) above the top of the cage. Incandescent lights should be at least 6 in (15 cm) above the top of the cage.

In addition to allowing the animal to thermoregulate, basking behavior serves another important function for the chameleon. The sun's ultraviolet rays are converted into vitamin D_3, which most animals need for absorbing calcium from their digestive tracts. Gravid females commonly exhibit increased basking behavior, especially in the final weeks before laying. This may be a way to produce additional D_3 to meet the calcium demands of their developing eggs. The most frequent nutritional deficiency encountered in captive *C. c. calyptratus* is a vitamin D_3 deficiency. Without D_3, calcium is not absorbed, leading to metabolic bone deficiencies (MBD). To resolve the D_3 issue, you must provide proper lighting sources with sufficient levels of UVB. When purchasing the fluorescent bulbs, make sure they are of a UVB type. I have used Zoo Med ReptiSun UVB 5.0 bulbs for years, but there are many similar type bulbs available.

Feeding

Like most chameleon species, veiled chameleons eat crickets, locusts, grasshoppers, flies, mealworms, roaches, wax worms, silkworms, and almost any type of insect presented to them. *C. c. calyptratus* is truly omnivorous (it eats both plant material and insects and other small lizards as well). It may be surprising to some people that the chameleon's diet should include some plant matter along with insects. However, the objective for the hobbyist is to provide the chameleon with a feeding regime that closely parallels its diet in nature. In Yemen, there is a very distinct rainy season. In the rainy season there is an increase of insects as well as available water. However, during the dry periods, the veiled

A veiled chameleon catches a cricket for dinner.

chameleon must turn to alternative food and water sources. During the dry periods, the ingestion of plant matter acts as a supplemental food and water resource for this chameleon's survival.

Offering fresh vegetables to chameleons is not as odd as one would think. Many chameleons have been observed consuming various forms of vegetation. The types of items you can offer vary from nontoxic leaves and flowers to cut-up greens and spinach, broccoli bits, grated carrots, and small pieces of fresh fruit (grapes, berries, and similar fruits) offered in a small bowl. Another alternative is to provide the small flats of seedling romaine lettuce or other greens that are available at any garden supply store. Just make sure that they are pesticide free before you place them in the cage.

Another alternative is a pot of live hibiscus. Both the plant and the flowers are edible as well as decorative, plus they have the bonus of providing additional vitamin C. Offering young *C. c. calyptratus* alfalfa sprouts and pureed vegetable baby food is another way to give them a source of vegetable matter in their diet. Place the baby food directly onto the leaves of the plants in the cage, and the chameleons will just lick it off.

Initially, there may not be a rush to consume these offerings, but if you slow down on the quantity and availability of the insects, you will see increased interest in the noninsect food items. Insects should be the major part of the diet, but they should not be provided exclusively. The insects should be offered every other day to the adults. Adults should be fed twelve large crickets or five to six super worms or wax worms every other day. Juveniles should be fed twelve to twenty small crickets every day. Place the insects inside a small glass bowl inside the cage.

Remember that most commercially available insects are low in calcium and high in phosphorous. The need for a vitamin and mineral supplementation is clearly indicated. Supplementation can be done by dusting the insects with a variety of powdered vitamin and mineral products for reptiles offered in a twice-weekly rotation. These products are available at most pet supply stores.

Watering

There are many methods of delivering water to your chameleon. Most chameleons will not drink from a bowl of water. Instead, mist the plants, and provide a drip system of some type. There are several products available that make it easy to install a home drip system. A drip system consists of a container fitted with an on-off valve. A small piece of tubing is attached to the container, and the container is filled with water. The valve is adjusted to regulate the flow so that it slowly drips into the cage and onto the plant leaves. This dip combined with a misting of the cage foliage twice a day should be more than enough to meet the hydration needs of *C. c. calyptratus*.

CHAPTER 10

REPRODUCTION

Wait for a chameleon to reach its full adult growth before considering reproduction. This is a responsible approach to breeding. The chameleon is given the time to fully develop, and the reproductive risks of compromising a partially grown reptile are significantly reduced. The age, size, and health of a female should always be considered carefully before deciding whether to breed her. The breeding size of an adult female should average between 12 and 16 in (30.5 and 40.6 cm) in overall length. The female should be somewhere between ten and fourteen months old when she is first bred. A male can be bred earlier, as reproduction does not place the demands on his body that it does on the female. However, I highly recommend that a male also be allowed to reach full adult growth before breeding because the demands of courtship and reproducing are all stressful for the chameleon. It is always best to have a fully mature reptile for breeding.

In full color, a gravid veiled chameleon indicates she is pregnant and therefore unreceptive to males.

Provided you have a mature and healthy pair, mating and reproduction is the next step in most chameleon owners' goals of captive husbandry. Always introduce the male into a female's enclosure for the purpose of mating rather than the other way around. Male chameleons are territorial, and a male chameleon will be aggressive toward a female if she is brought into his enclosure. One method to test for compatibility is to set the cages up within view of each other and see how the two chameleons respond to each other. If the colorations on both indicate interest, proceed with an introduction. Once initial mating begins, the danger of aggression by the male decreases significantly; however, the mating pair should be watched closely for signs of undue aggression by the male and separated if necessary.

When to attempt mating is ultimately regulated by the receptivity of the female. The coloration of the female is the key to successfully assuring that it is the time to attempt an introduction for mating. The basic day-to-day coloration of a *C. c. calyptratus* female is a light green with horizontal rows of white patches and sometimes orange or yellow elongated spots. (There are always some variations in the basic coloration from chameleon to chameleon.) The mating colors of a female *C. c. calyptratus* are the same as their passive colors with one important difference: When receptive to mating, females will usually, but not always, display aqua spotting along the back and tail with vertical streaks of the same color on the casque. Smaller blue spots will occur laterally farther down on the sides of her body. Other signs that a female is receptive will be clear once a male is introduced. If the female is receptive, she will remain in her mating colors or nonstress coloration. If the female is not in a receptive state, upon immediate sight of a male she will turn a dark green or black with bright blue and yellow orange spots, expand her gular area, curl her tail, flatten her body, and rock from side to side on her perch. If the male is close enough, she will usually gape fiercely at him and may even attempt to bite him.

The coloration of an adult male *C. c. calyptratus* when he views a female will change in much the same way as it

This young male veiled chameleon displays intensified coloration in hope of attracting a female.

does when he catches sight of another male. His coloration will intensify, and he will flatten his rib cage, expand his gular area, and roll up his tail. He will then begin nodding his head from side to side with a quick stop-jerk motion while approaching the female with a slightly rocking gait. If she is receptive, she may slowly begin to crawl away while maintaining her green coloration. The male will begin to follow her and may even butt his snout against her hips with his mouth closed. He will slowly approach her, crawling onto her back to position himself for mating. The act of mating lasts several minutes and may occur more than once during the day.

Anywhere from eighteen hours to three days after a successful copulation, the female will begin to reject the male. This will be demonstrated by a display of gravid coloration (the dark green-black with aqua and yellow-orange spotting). You should separate the chameleons at this point. It is important to understand that a female who has successfully mated will usually display gravid colors only in the presence of a male (and possibly another female) but may continue to display normal coloration in her unstressed state.

Egg Laying

Females will lay their eggs 30 to 40 days after mating (or 90 to 120 days after their last oviposition if there are multiple clutches from a single mating). The clutch sizes of wild *C. c. calyptratus* are much smaller than those of captive

This gravid veiled chameleon will oviposit her eggs thirty to forty days after mating.

females, ranging from ten to twenty eggs. I believe that key environmental factors in their natural habitat are responsible for regulating clutch size. The seasonal temperature fluctuation and the cyclical abundance of a certain plant or food prey they consume have direct effects on egg production. In captivity, the abundance of food and buffering of seasonal influences have changed the reproductive mode from a chameleon that produces a small annual clutch to one that produces large multiple clutches one after the other. The result is that often females in captivity do not live beyond their fifth or sixth clutch. This is surely due to the stresses caused by the extremely large clutch sizes of captive animals, which sometimes reach three to four times those of wild females.

In the final weeks of development, the maturing eggs may account for more than half of the animal's total body weight. Somewhere around three to five days before laying her eggs, the female *C. c. calyptratus* will usually stop eating and become restless, possibly climbing about the cage and exploring areas near the bottom of the enclosure. When these behaviors are observed, they indicate that the female is nearing the time to lay her eggs and should be moved to a nesting site.

There are two options for providing a nesting site for the female. You can place a container or tub filled with moist soil or clean sand in the cage with her, or you can use a nesting container such as a 33-gallon (125-liter) plastic trash can. The bottom of the container should be lined with at least 4 to 6 in (10 to 15 cm) of substrate moistened enough to hold a formed tunnel (but not wet). The soil should be tamped down so it will hold the tunnel shape without collapsing. At oviposition, a female *C. c. calyptratus* will dig a tunnel at a 45- to 50-degree angle, using her front claws to loosen the soil and her back feet to move the loosened soil out of the burrow. She will then back herself almost completely into the tunnel with only her nose visible and lay her eggs very rapidly. Once all eggs have been laid, she will turn around and pack the tunnel, again using primarily her front feet. When she has done this, she is ready to be returned to her cage and offered some water and food.

The next step is to unearth the eggs and set them up for incubation. *C. c. calyptratus* eggs are oval shaped and range in weight from 1 to 1.5 grams. The eggs range from 8 to 9 mm in width and from 15 to 17 mm in length. Newly laid eggs can be left buried for a few hours or removed immediately after oviposition. When you do excavate the nest, carefully remove the soil from the eggs. When you get to the eggs, gently move them onto a paper towel until you place them into the incubation container.

Incubation of Eggs

Once the eggs are excavated, place them in an incubator. This is a container that is partially filled with moderately moist, but not wet, vermiculite, perlite, sphagnum moss, or peat moss as the incubation medium. If you use vermiculite,

Immediately after they have been laid, eggs should be excavated and placed in an incubator.

slowly moisten it until it clumps together when you grab a handful. It should not be so wet that water would drip if it were squeezed tightly. If you use perlite, mix 1.5 parts perlite with no more than 1 part water by weight.

After filling the container with incubation medium, there should still be space left for the hatchlings to occupy once they hatch. Place the eggs on their side, partially buried in the moistened incubation medium. Leave 40 to 50 percent of the egg surface exposed, and space the eggs 1 inch (2.5 cm) or less apart from each other (but not touching).

Cover the container opening with a lid or with plastic wrap secured by a rubber band. Punch two or three pin-size holes in the lid or plastic wrap. You can also use a Tupperware-like container with a dozen or so pinholes made in the lid.

Incubate the eggs at 78°F (26°C) during the day, with a nightly temperature drop to a low of 74°F (23°C). The eggs will hatch in approximately five to nine months. Check the eggs every two to three weeks. If the medium feels dry, add more water in small amounts until the desired moisture level is achieved. Discard any eggs that are molding or infertile.

There is some speculation among private breeders that there may be a correlation between incubation temperatures and sex determination. The idea is that higher incubation temperatures will produce more males and lower ones produce more females. This needs to be explored further as it could be very helpful to the hobbyist with breeding programs.

The Veiled Hatchlings

When the eggs are about to hatch, small water beads will form on the egg surfaces (often referred to as sweating). Anywhere from two to fifteen hours later, the hatchlings will start to slit the egg using the egg tooth on the tip of their snouts. They will use this tooth to make crisscrossing star-shape slits at one end of the egg. After slitting the egg, they may remain in the egg for another ten to fifteen hours while they absorb any remaining egg yolk. Be patient; let the hatchlings emerge on their own.

Once the eggs are slit, the hatchlings may wait up to fifteen hours before they emerge.

The hatchlings should measure anywhere from 2.1 to 3 in (5.3 to 7.6 cm) in length (from nose tip to tail tip). With close inspection, male hatchlings are distinguishable from females at birth by their heel spurs, which are absent in females. Hatchlings should be carefully cleaned of any clinging substrate and placed into a fine-screened cage with appropriate-size branches and plants. It is of key importance that *C. c. calyptratus* hatchlings be reared in an enclosure that has good ventilation. They can be housed in groups, but be sure to watch for any aggression.

This hatchling veiled chameleon can be placed in a cage with other hatchlings (but watch for aggression) or be raised by itself.

The hatchlings may begin eating immediately or wait as long as two days. The hatchlings fare best on fruit flies and two-week-old crickets, about a dozen each day, until the hatchlings are about 8 in (20.3 cm) in length. Offer young *C. c. calyptratus* alfalfa sprouts and pureed vegetable baby food; this is an excellent way to give them a source of fruit and vegetable matter in their diet. The baby food can be placed on the leaves of the plants in their cage for them to lick off the leaves. It will also entice the fruit flies and crickets that may be loose in the cage, so the little chameleons get a double treat.

Breeding Concerns

We need to be more responsible in our breeding of *C. c. calyptratus*. A rush to reproduce these reptiles before they have properly matured and uncontrolled breeding, as well as bad husbandry, have contributed to serious physical defects and premature deaths.

A history of misinformation and misconceptions have caused these chameleons to be bred much too early and too often. In the early 1990s, when veiled chameleons were first imported, one of the buzz phrases about them was "baby to baby in one year." These chameleons appeared very hardy and easy to reproduce. The initial prices were fairly high, but the idea that they were easy to breed created a lucrative market.

Along with the rush to reproduce the species at a very young age came rumors that a zoo was experiencing a die-off of subadult female veiled chameleons prior to breeding. Over time, these stories evolved into the myth that the females must breed or die, which led to more premature and too-frequent breeding.

Had people stopped to consider the long-term implications of the die-off theory, they would have known it was unreasonable. The basic objective of reproduction is to make sure that the species continues, so designing a female chameleon to be an all-or-nothing creature defeats this objective. In a breed-or-die scenario, it wouldn't take long for *C. c. calyptratus* to disappear altogether.

Although this baby veiled chameleon, like the rest of its species, will develop rapidly, it should not be bred until it is fully mature.

In reality, the *Chamaeleo* species have evolved with such reproductive efficiency that they have the ability, once bred, to retain sperm, assuring continued reproduction even without a mate present. In addition, it's clear that female veiled chameleons do not have to breed immediately to survive. One long-term breeder of *C. c. calyptratus* maintained female veiled chameleons well into their third and fourth year without breeding them. They were healthy, viable chameleons.

Pushing these chameleons to quickly grow and reproduce has taken a toll on the species as a whole. Females in the wild typically produce an annual clutch of eggs that numbers between fourteen and the low twenties. In captivity, in response to the fecundity of food and water, females have a higher and quicker reproductive rate. They have been reported to produce as high as eighty-plus eggs in a clutch, while cycling clutches one after the other. Think of the physical demands such a huge difference place on a female that produces that many eggs over and over. Some breeders report females that were so heavy with eggs that they could not move off the floor of their enclosures. In the wild, this is inconceivable. If a wild female was confined to the ground, she would most likely end up being a predator's meal.

Another reproduction concern for *C. c. calyptratus* is the ongoing perception among chameleon breeders that they are inbred and genetically defective. Are we really seeing genetic problems or a chameleon being pushed past its limits? We push these chameleons to grow and reproduce in large numbers. Then we blame the chameleon because it can't handle the demand put upon it, leading to malformations, weakness, poor hatch rates, and sudden death.

In my opinion, the main defects observed in *C. c. calyptratus* are the result of improper captive husbandry. In the wild, they have proven their ability to thrive in less than ideal conditions. An ongoing lack of available food and water and extremes in temperature indicate that they are very hardy.

Many people have associated the malformation of bone development in veiled chameleons as a genetic problem. However, the usual cause of this is improper supplementa-

A baby veiled lounges on the crest of an adult male. Contrary to what many people believe, this species is not naturally plagued with genetic defects. Problems such as bone malformations can be traced to bad husbandry of captive reptiles.

tion and lighting, not genetics. If a reptile is pushed to grow quickly, the necessary vitamins and minerals may not be available or assimilated for proper bone growth and formation. This condition is termed metabolic bone disorder, or MBD. Without proper amounts of vitamin D_3, the chameleon cannot properly absorb calcium. The result is a softening of the bones that manifests in bowed legs, drooping casques, fracturing of the ribs, and overall bone loss and malformation. The source for vitamin D_3 is through supplementation and a proper lighting source. Natural sunlight is the ideal source for D_3 (UVB). There also are excellent forms of UVB-containing artificial lighting that can effectively provide an alternative source to natural sunlight.

We can take responsibility to produce healthy veiled chameleons by not pushing them to grow too quickly, by limiting their reproduction, and by ensuring they receive adequate nutrition and D_3. We can also take responsibility in the area of natural selection. In nature, only the strongest survive. In captivity, we have a great buffering effect on the process of natural selection. We must make sure to breed only the best examples of veiled chameleons and allow the remaining chameleons to only be kept as pets. This is a common practice in many areas of animal reproduction. Reputable dog breeders allow only dogs of show quality to be bred. Other dogs are sold with restricted papers, requiring the owner to spay or neuter the dog. While this won't work with reptiles, the overall practice is sound and the intention is valid.

The fact that thousands of veiled chameleons have been reproduced in captivity is a testament to their durability and adaptation. Now we need to fully assess their husbandry needs in captivity.

Conclusion

Big, bold, and beautiful, *Chamaeleo calyptratus calyptratus* is probably the most widely held species. A truly stunning chameleon with its high casque, spectacular coloration, and size, it is a species that demands attention. The intention of this chapter is to help with our continued understanding of this unique species' captive requirements and to suggest we still have much more to learn.

Acknowledgments

I would like to express my love and gratitude to my mother, Dorothy Kalisch, for her ongoing love and understanding, which have allowed me to foster and explore my endless love for all the flora and fauna I have had the joy to have experienced in my life.

Among the hardiest of chameleons, veiled chameleons such as this one make excellent pets. However, producing healthy ones means taking the time to understand their needs and provide them with the proper care.

PART IV

Parson's Chameleon
(*Calumma parsonii parsonii*)

By Kenneth Kalisch

CHAPTER 11

INTRODUCTION AND NATURAL HISTORY

If one species of chameleon should be chosen as the representative for the entire chameleon group, the large and majestic Parson's chameleon deserves to be the top choice. Originally described as *Cameleonis rariss* in 1768 by James Parsons and identified and renamed in honor of Parsons by G. Cuvier in 1824, Parson's chameleon (*Calumma parsonii parsonii*) is one of the largest Malagasy species of the Chamaeleonidae family.

Males have been recorded to a maximum size of 27.75 in (70.5 cm) total length (16-in [40.5-cm] snout-to-vent length) and females to a maximum size of 19.75 in (50 cm) total length (11.75-in [30-cm] snout-to-vent length). There have been reports of males that exceeded 29 in (33.5 cm) in total length, which would supersede the size of the purported largest chameleon species, *Furcifer oustaleti.*

Common Name: Parson's chameleon

Latin name: *Chamaeleo parsonii* (Cuvier, 1824)
Reclassified: *Calumma parsonii parsonii* (Klaver and Bohme, 1986)
Nominate form: *Calumma parsonii parsonii* (Cuvier, 1824)
Subspecies: *Calumma parsonii cristifer* (Methuen and Hewitt, 1913)

Males have a green to turquoise blue ground cover with three or four brownish, slightly curved diagonal stripes that stretch from the dorsum toward the anterior of the body. At the center of each flank is a pale yellow-white spot. (This spot varies in size and is sometimes completely absent from one side or both flanks.) The eye turrets are large and can be

This good-size chameleon is a female Parson's chameleon (*Calumma parsonii parsonii*), one of the largest Malagasy species of the Chamaeleonidae family.

a clear yellow to a deep copper orange. Females are predominantly a uniform green varying from a yellow-green to a bluish green. They have the same diagonal striping as the males do, although the stripes are much less pronounced in females. The center flank spot is also variable. The squamation (scale arrangement) is homogeneous and smooth, formed of quadrangular scales. The male has a paired divergent rostral process, which is often verrucose (warty) and denticulated at its edge; the female has none. Both sexes have occipital lobes that appear as folds of approximately ⅛ in (3 mm) at the posterior of the head. They possess no dorsal or ventral crest.

The color variations of *C. p. parsonii* are more evident in the males. The common terms used to describe the variations are self-explanatory, for example: *yellow-lipped*, *yellow*, *orange*, and *green-eyed* forms. In females, the color variations are subtle, usually confined to muted undertones of blue or yellow, although an occasional dark tan has been seen. These represent geographic color variations. Stress coloration in the males is a general overall color blanching or darkening, showing dark brown to black diagonal stripes with dark spotting scattered over the body. Females that are stressed display an increase in yellow color, which shows as spots or blotches. When this coloration reaches its peak, the female appears to be yellow with green spotting.

Calumma parsonii cristifer, a subspecies of the Parson's chameleon, has some distinct differences from the nominate form. The subspecies is smaller, with males reaching 19 in (48.3 cm) total length (10.5-in [26.5-cm] snout-to-vent length). Females reach 15.75 in (40 cm) total length (8.75-in [22.2-cm] snout-to-vent length). Both sexes have a dorsal crest that is distinct over the first half to two-thirds of the body, formed of small, regular conical tubercles. Another distinguishing feature is a small parietal crest. Coloration of the males consists of variations of blue-green with a rust orange blotch on the flanks. A pale yellow-white spot may be found in the center of each flank. Females are a green to brown with a rust orange blotch on the flank. They may also have the pale yellow-white spot in the center of each flank. *C. p. cristifer's* classification as a subspecies of *C. p. parsonii* is in need of further research as it appears to be more closely aligned with the species *C. oshaughnessyi oshaughnessyi*, adding to the confusion with identification and localities of *C. p. parsonii* and *C. p. cristifer*.

C. p. parsonii's habitat of preference is in the primary rain forest. Its range is predominantly in the montane forests in the eastern zone of Madagascar. It is reported to be found from the north in Montagne d'Ambre to as far south as Fort Dauphin. It has also been found on the eastern island of Nosy Boraha and is reported to be on the north-western island of Nosy Bé and in Ambanja on the west coast

As this photograph and the previous one demonstrate, the coloring of male Parson's chameleons is more dramatic than that of the females. This lizard has the typical color and patterning of the Parson's male, including brownish diagonal stripes and a pale yellow-white spot.

of Madagascar. However, the identifications for Montagne d'Ambre, Nosy Bé, and Ambanja are probably misidentifications of two somewhat similar species, *C. oshaughnessyi ambreensis* and *C. oshaughnessyi oshaughnessyi*. Rainfall in their habitat is plentiful as well as variable, depending on seasons and localities. The east coast has the highest annual rainfall on the island. *C. p. parsonii* is more commonly found at moderate to higher altitudes but is also found at sea level.

C. p. cristifer is found in a limited range of the eastern zone of rain forest and does not overlap into the range of *C. p. parsonii*. The sole location for *C. p. cristifer* is Perinet (Andasibe). Rainfall is approximately 67 in (170.2 cm) per year. This subspecies is found at altitudes of 2,600 to 4,200 ft (800 to 1,300 m).

The habitats of *C. p. parsonii* and *C. p. cristifer*, for the most part, are confined to the eastern forests. The best way of understanding the environmental variations is to give an overview of the basic localities, physical ranges, and rainfall variations within the range of the Parson's chameleon, moving from north to south. The rainfall of Madagascar is heaviest in the eastern region, diminishing as it moves west as well as from northern to southern localities. The temperature basically follows the same pattern. Coastline temperatures are the warmest, with the temperatures dropping as one moves east and as elevation increases. (The temperature pattern reverts once past the high massif, and temperatures start to increase as one moves into the western region of the island.) The humidity is high, varying from 75 to 95 percent, depending on the time of year and rainfall, which on the east coast is fairly constant.

The physical and vegetative environment that the Parson's chameleon inhabits is divided into two basic types: the lowland evergreen forests and the high-altitude montane forests. The lowland forest canopy reaches approximately 100 ft (30 m) and is noteworthy in that it is composed of a very diverse tree population as well as ferns, palms, epiphytes, and bamboo. As one moves up in altitude and into the montane rain forest, the canopy lowers to

Pictured is a Parson's chameleon in its natural habitat in East Madagascar.

around 65 to 80 ft (20 to 25 m). The trees branch closer to their bases in a more horizontal direction, thus creating fewer vertical trunks. There is an abundance of tree ferns, mosses, and lichens as well as a large variety of other fern species. *C. p. parsonii* inhabits the remaining vestiges of original forest and areas of secondary growth and the fringe areas of deforested regions. It is even found to inhabit areas within villages. The fact that deforestation has left only 5 to 7 percent of the original forest surely threatens their range and has forced them into close quarters with humans. Parson's chameleons have also been observed inhabiting corridors of Malagasy's agricultural areas near sea level; they were found living in areas lushly planted with large breadfruit and mango trees as well as on coffee plants growing below these trees.

The behaviors of *C. p. parsonii* are remarkable in the sense that they are fairly slothlike in their movements. Unlike most of the *Chamaeleo* species, which are active throughout the day, Parson's chameleons are sedentary for long periods. This chameleon will find a spot on a branch that suits it, and as long as water, food, and temperatures permit, it will commonly remain there for several days. If the environmental factors are constant, the lizard's main motivation for movement is defecation, usually once or twice per week in mature specimens. This activity consists of moving through their environment, drinking, eating, defecating, and either returning to the original roosting spot or choosing another.

The other obvious motive for an increase in the activity levels of the Parson's chameleon is to reproduce. The behavior exhibited in relationship to reproduction (especially significant in the male) is active for this species. The courtship is signaled by the male's intensification of coloration and the initiation of head nodding. The nodding consists of a rolling jerk, moving right to left. As the male approaches the female, the nodding continues. If the female is receptive, the male will mount her, and copulation occurs. The copulation can last ten to thirty minutes. If the female is not receptive, she will display yellow spotting, flatten her body laterally, extend the gular sac, and rock from side to side. If this display does not discourage the male's advances, she will turn overall yellow and open her mouth and may even charge the pursuing male.

When males encounter each other, they exhibit lateral flattening, gular extension, and blanching of coloration but no rocking motion. In place of the rocking behavior, males will straighten their legs, extend their tails, raise them up over their backs, and as their tails descend, roll them up.

By displaying yellow spotting, this female Parson's chameleon warns males that she is unreceptive to copulation.

This display repeats as they approach each other. As with other *Chamaeleo* species, this is a ritual to establish or defend territory or reproductive rights. It is theorized that this behavior may in part trigger the onset of reproduction. The males face off and may butt heads a few times. Typically, the end result is the retreat of the submissive or defeated male. It is extremely rare for males to cause physical harm to each other, but always use caution with new introductions in captivity.

Range Sample of Reported East Coast Locales of *C. p. parsonii* and *C. p. cristifer*

LOCATION	ALTITUDES	ANNUAL RAINFALL	TEMPERATURE
Montagne d' Ambre (north)	2,789–4,835 ft (850–1,474.5 m)	141+ in (358+ cm)	54°F–80°F (12°C–26°C)
Marojejy	2,600–4,750 ft (800–1,448 m)	118+ in (300+ cm)	59°F–84°F (15°C–29°C)
Perinet Range of: *C. p. cristifer*	2,600–4,625 ft (792–1,410 m)	67+ in (170+ cm)	37°F–73°F (3°C–23°C)
Nosy Boraha	Sea level to +/–1000 ft (+/–340 m)	130 in (330 cm)	59°F–84°F (15°C–29°C)
Ranomafana	2,625–3,937 ft (800–1,200 m)	102+ in (259+ cm)	43°F–76°F (6°C–24°C)
Andringitra	2,300–5,000 ft (700–1,524 m)	79+ in (200+ cm)	34°F–75°F (1°C–24°C)
Andohahela (south)	2,300–6,417 ft (700–1,956 m)	79+ in (200+ cm)	43°F–74°F (6°C–23°C)

CHAPTER 12

CAPTIVE CARE

Parson's chameleons are no longer imported or sold in pet stores; you must buy captive-bred chameleons through private breeders. The cost is prohibitive, about $2,500-plus for one Parson's chameleon. As when buying any chameleon, always buy from a breeder with a good reputation. Do not buy animals that look sickly or undernourished. Take your new chameleon to see a qualified reptile veterinarian as soon as possible so it can be treated for any parasites and given a clean bill of health.

Husbandry

With a basic understanding of the Parson's chameleon's natural environment and behaviors, it is possible to apply this information to four areas of captive care.

- Housing: This is a large species that needs a large cage in which it feels at ease.
- Water: It comes from regions with heavy rainfall and high humidity and needs an abundant water supply.

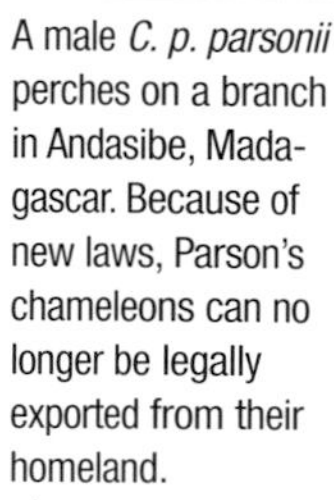

A male *C. p. parsonii* perches on a branch in Andasibe, Madagascar. Because of new laws, Parson's chameleons can no longer be legally exported from their homeland.

Good husbandry with a Parson's chameleon such as this female means re-creating its native habitat as closely as possible in the captive environment.

- Temperature and light: The regions that this species frequents are moderate to cool; keep temperatures below 85°F (29°C). Parson's chameleon comes from shaded areas of deep forest and requires indirect filtered light.
- Food: Because of its size, it prefers larger insect forms.

Using these four elements as guides, let's take each one and apply it to captive care. It is important to stress that these elements are interdependent. They are an artificial attempt to re-create, as closely as possible, the natural conditions in which the Parson's chameleons are found to increase the likelihood of success in captive management.

Housing and Furniture

One of the more important aspects of captive care is the enclosure that your chameleon(s) will dwell in. The Parson's chameleon is a large species and in the wild inhabits a large territory. It should be housed singly in as large a cage as possible. The minimum size cage for a single lizard is 4 ft long × 4 ft wide × 4 ft high (122 cm × 122 cm ×122 cm). The enclosure should be made of ½-inch to 1-inch (1.3-cm to 2.5-cm) screening that is vinyl coated (to protect the chameleons if they crawl on the screening). It is also important to place the cage at the proper height; the top should be

The Parson's chameleon requires a large, heavily planted enclosure.

around 6 ft (1.8 m) from the ground. You may need to place the cage on a table or cabinet to achieve this height.

The interior of the cage needs to contain an abundance of foliage and branches. Parson's chameleon comes from dense forest, so provide as much cover as possible to give the lizard a better sense of security. This can be accomplished with the use of potted nontoxic plants such as *Ficus benjamina*, *Schefflera arboricola*, and ferns and hanging plants such as orchids, bromeliads, pothos, philodendron, and ivy. The goal is to create an environment that provides privacy and security.

The branches should be of the proper size and placed in predominantly horizontal modes. Choose branches of varying circumference with a textured surface to facilitate the chameleon's grip. Be sure that the branch circumference is slightly larger than the grip of the reptile's feet. The foliage and branches should not be so dense that the lizard's ability to navigate through the cage is impaired. There should be a balance of planting, with a lacework of branches, and within this, open areas.

Feeding

You are what you eat and chameleons are no different. A chameleon's diet corresponds to its overall heath and reproduction. Much has been written about food types and supplementation for chameleons, and much has been recently discovered in that area of husbandry. However, we still have a long way to go. The problem that faces any chameleon keeper is reproducing a diet that will fulfill the animal's nutritional needs as it would in the wild. This is no easy task.

The most common food prey in Parson's chameleon's natural environment are locusts, grasshoppers, butterflies, cockroaches, mantises, stick insects, moths, and assorted flies. I have observed that Parson's chameleons will occasionally eat small birds, rodents, and lizards as well. Providing this food list in captivity would be fairly intimidating. Nevertheless, it is possible to provide them with a varied diet. This means that the herpetologist will need to expand his or her duties to include some basic entomology and begin to propagate insects. There are several species of cockroaches that are easily cultured. The two most commonly available—*Blaberus craniifer* (death's head cockroach) and *Gromphadorhina portentosa* (hissing cockroach)—are excellent larger food sources. *Blaberus craniifer*, being the more prolific of the two, is a good starting point. Other commercially available insects are crickets, super worms, silkworms, wax worms, butter worms, and mealworms. Adult chameleons should be offered twelve large crickets and two or three large cockroaches every other day. Juveniles should be offered about a dozen crickets every day. The nutritional value of any of these insects can be improved through nutrient loading, or gut loading, them by

Climbing branches should be placed horizontally within the cage.

feeding them rolled oats, ground legumes, cornmeal, fresh greens, carrots, sweet potatoes, apples, and oranges. Collecting insects from the wild can provide additional insects, as long as it is done in areas known to be pesticide free. Another way to improve the insects' nutritional value is to dust insects with a vitamin-mineral supplement. (There are a number of commercially available supplements made for reptiles.) Do this twice a week. You also may add liquid bird vitamins to the lizards' drinking water once a month.

Watering and Humidity

The natural environment that *C. p. parsonii* inhabits has an abundance of rainfall. This has a twofold effect: high levels of humidity and a fairly consistent supply of drinking water. Parson's are heavy, slow, and long drinkers. A thirsty Parson's can drink for as long as forty-five minutes. Provide a watering device with a regular slow drip. This can be accomplished in many ways. The simplest method is to place a container with a pinhole in the bottom of it on top of the cage. There are also commercially available drip containers made specifically for this purpose. Depending on the size of the container, it will supply a constant drip for as long as several hours.

A male yellow-lip morph of Parson's chameleon drinks water. These chameleons require regular watering.

Other means of supplying water can be as elaborate as a timer-misting-drip system (which can be set to mist or drip several times a day) or as simple as installing a drip container and misting the foliage in the cage with a spray bottle. Whatever you choose, the lizards need to be given a fairly substantial amount of water on a daily basis. The goal is to provide enough water for drinking and humidity but still allow the environment to dry out between applications of water. An ever-present supply of water or wetness can increase the growth of harmful bacteria and fungi, so monitor these levels carefully. A good practice is to supply the lizards with a drip container in the morning and mist the foliage. Then mist the foliage again in the late afternoon or early evening. Unless your climate is unusually dry, this should be adequate. If the humidity is low, a relatively simple solution is to purchase a cool-air humidifier available at drugstores for $30 to $45, which will increase the humidity without overwatering the cage.

Lighting and Heating

C. p. parsonii specimens are found in deeply shaded habitat. They typically inhabit areas within dense foliage. Their environment is high in humidity, with heavy amounts of rainfall. Thus they probably do not encounter an abundance of direct sun; at most they get filtered sun. They are not known as heliophilic in the traditional sense as are Panther

In the wild, Parson's chameleons, such as this *C.p. cristifer*, are used to filtered sunlight.

chameleons, which bask laterally. Parson's chameleons will sun themselves for warmth, but it is uncommon for them to bask for extended periods of time.

In an indoor cage, it is important to provide them with both incandescent and fluorescent light sources. The incandescent lights provide warming spots as well as help dry the cage out between watering. The fluorescent lights provide light for the lizards and have the additional benefit of assisting plant growth. The fluorescent lighting should be the main source of light, creating the appropriate levels of brightness without increasing the temperature. The type of fluorescent bulbs used should contain UVB to assist in the proper absorption of calcium. The lights should be placed outside the cage, either on top or to the side. They should be at least 6 in (15 cm) away from the cage.

C. p. parsonii comes from an environment that has a much wider range of temperatures than one might expect. Because of the altitude and seasonal variance, it can range from the low 40s F (4.5°C–6 °C) to the mid 80s °F (28°C–30°C), with the average temperature hovering around 73°F (23°C). As the east coast of Madagascar enters winter, the higher elevations (which are cooler to begin with) go through a significant drop in temperature. The Parson's in these areas respond by going into a dormant phase. The temperature reduction has a direct effect on their activity levels as well as on their feeding and drinking patterns. They will find a specific place on a branch and stay there, sometimes for weeks, moving occasionally to feed or to defecate. During this time, they may eat only an occasional insect, and their water intake is slowed.

Through the dormancy, the lizards' weight should be monitored by periodic weighing of them. There should be no appreciable weight loss. If there is a substantial change in weight, the temperature should be gradually increased and feeding should resume. In captivity, it is extremely important to make certain that the lizards are in optimum health and are well acclimated before attempting a cooling down. The first effort is to provide them with a comfortable temperature range from 68°F to 80°F (20°C to 27°C) before exposing them to lower temperatures. The most common mistake keepers make is to keep Parson's chameleons at too-high temperatures. Higher temperatures can stress their systems and result in respiratory problems or other complications. Similar problems occur in *Chamaeleo* species from montane climates when they are kept at elevated temperatures. Allowing time for your lizard to adjust will be beneficial to its health and reproduction in the long run. Before attempting to cool your chameleon, consult a reptile veterinarian or experienced breeder.

The Four Elements

Creating a balance between the four elements of husbandry—housing, feeding, watering, and heating and lighting—is the challenge for Parson's chameleon keepers. The objective is to create a sizable, well-planted environment with the proper amount of humidity, water, food, and light and acceptable temperatures.

CHAPTER 13

REPRODUCTION

For the most part, the reproduction of Parson's chameleons is still in the stages of discovery. Parson's chameleons depart from typical chameleon reproduction in that they appear to be annual breeders. They also have a longer gestation and incubation of their eggs than do other chameleons.

Parson's lay their eggs in soil 6 to 10 in (15 to 25.5 cm) deep. Incubation of the eggs is handled in the same manner as that of other chameleons. The incubation should have a slight temperature variation, with the temperatures not exceeding 74°F (23°C). Eggs have been recorded hatching anywhere from twelve to twenty-four months.

Sexing of Parson's is simple in adults as they are sexually dimorphic. Females are smaller with more uniform coloring. Males have a divergent rostral process (horns), while the female has none. However, it can be quite difficult to sex Parson's chameleons under one year of age.

Because of its age, this juvenile Parson's (photographed at the Perinet Reserve in Madagascar) is difficult to sex.

Male Parson's chameleons such as the one at top are larger than the females and have rostral horns. Females such as the one at bottom have more uniform coloring.

Personal Observations on Husbandry, Reproduction, Incubation, and Hatching

In the 1990s, when I got my original pair of Parson's chameleons, little was known about their captive care and reproduction. I was told they would never survive and would definitely not reproduce. Since then, I have observed, experimented with, and taken a lot of notes on Parson's chameleons. I made many changes in my methods along the way and greatly improved the health and breeding success with each generation. Here is the story of my first fifteen years of keeping and breeding Parson's chameleons.

My original pair of Parson's was purchased as newly imported young adults. The male was approximately 18 in (46 cm) total length and weighed 8.2 ounces (232 grams). The female was 14 in (35.5 cm) total length and weighed 7.9 ounces (224 grams). The pair was placed in an indoor cage 4 ft long × 3 ft wide × 6 ft high (1.2 m × .9 m × 1.8 m). The interior of the cage had several large ficus trees, schefflera trees, and hanging vines and a network of branches. The lighting consisted of two incandescent spots and a pair of 48-inch (1.2-meter) double fluorescent fixtures. Each fixture contained one plant light and one Vita-Lite (current recommendation is to use Zoo Med ReptiSun UVB 5.0 bulbs or bulbs with UVB). The lizards slowly adapted to their environment, eventually establishing their own specific perching and sleeping spots. The cage had a drip-cup system and was misted twice a day, morning and evening.

The Parson's chameleons seemed to drink regularly, but my initial concern was their lack of food intake. I offered them everything I had on hand—crickets, wax worms, mealworms, and butter worms—but they showed little interest. The next step was to procure other insect forms. *Blaberus* spp. were found and offered. The response was excellent, and both chameleons fed well. However, my dilemma was the cost and availability of the cockroaches. I then began collecting wild cabbage moths, and these became a favorite food for the chameleons but, like cockroaches, were a limited resource. A source of grasshoppers was finally found; although somewhat costly, they were regularly available. The chameleons generally ate four to six grasshoppers per day. With the food situation under control, the lizards' acclimation seemed to progress very well. In the next six months, I began to expand their diet to include a much wider variety of common insects. Within eight months, the weight of the male had increased by 6.5 ounces (185 grams) and the female by 5.1 ounces (145 grams).

At this point, everything appeared to be stable. The lizards had been checked by a veterinarian and were clean of parasites. The adjustment to captivity appeared positive. Their activity levels were fairly sedentary compared with other species with which I had worked, but I finally relaxed and accepted this as typical behavior. In the spring, I observed that the male was showing interest in breeding and that activity levels of the pair seemed to be increasing. The male began to pursue the female, nodding and attempting to approach her, but the female seemed indifferent. When the male approached her, she would move out of his reach but not much farther. I observed many attempts by the male to mount the female but no copulation.

This is an ideal outdoor cage for Parson's chameleons.

In early summer, the pair were moved to an 8 ft long × 4 ft wide × 7 ft high (2.4 m × 1.2 m × 2.1 m) outdoor enclosure with an earthen floor (the cage bottom was built into the ground) and planting and branch arrangements similar to those in the indoor cage. The cage had a drip system that was turned on daily for thirty to forty-five minutes. Both lizards easily made the adjustment to the outdoor enclosure. The temperature ranged from 68°F to 80°F (20°C to 27°C).

Over the next few weeks, the pattern of behavior for the pair appeared normal. During this time, the breeding displays by the male seemed to gradually subside, and the pair cohabited without incident. The male frequented the upper branches; the female usually occupied the midarea of the cage.

In mid-June, the female's food intake slowed and continued to diminish to an insect or two each week by mid-July. I began to think her health might be compromised, although she showed no visible signs of illness or stress. To investigate this possibility, I first weighed her. The results were not what I had expected. Her weight was several grams higher than it had been at the previous weighing. I also checked her for respiratory problems and parasites, but neither was present. I concluded at this point that she was in good health and simply going through a diminished eating phase. As mid-August approached, she started to show signs of weight loss. I decided to remove the male to a cage out of her view to determine if his presence caused her lack of interest in feeding, but she did not resume feeding. During the last week of August, the female became restless, moving about the cage, crawling on the sides, and showing signs of stress. Her coloration showed more yellow, especially on the eye turrets. On August 27, I entered the cage to do my routine cleaning and found three eggs on the dirt floor. The cause of the female's appetite loss was now clear.

Two sides of the cage were covered with shade cloth to provide more privacy because the cage was in partial view of other species of *Chamaeleo*. I placed an additional 6 cubic ft (0.2 cubic m) of potting soil on the cage bottom to provide a more acceptable medium for the female to dig a nesting site. The following day, I found three more eggs on the bottom of the cage. The female was continuing her movement through the cage but made no attempt to dig. Another day passed, with no additional eggs and no indication of digging. On the fourth day, the female was moved to the indoor cage she had originally inhabited and was given an intramuscular injection (in the shoulder) at 11:30 a.m. of .03 mg of oxytocin to induce egg laying. The female positioned herself on a branch midpoint in the cage. At 12.25 p.m., she began to show signs of discomfort and took on a crouching stance with her vent averted to the side and her tail coiled around the branch. An egg appeared at 12:45 p.m., and as the process of egg laying (dropping) went on, she moved slowly through the lower and midsections of the cage, maintaining a stationary position for a few minutes prior to oviposition. The eggs were released approximately every fifteen to twenty-five minutes for a total of twenty-nine eggs after labor was induced, bringing the total number of eggs to thirty-five.

The female appeared thin. Her pre-oviposition weight had been 11.4 ounces (323 grams); her postgravid weight was 8.9 ounces (252 grams), putting her total weight loss at 3.9 ounces (111 grams) from her pregravid weight of 13 ounces (369 grams), with 2.4 ounces (68 grams) of the weight being the eggs. Her food intake resumed slowly two days after oviposition, and within two months she had regained 50 percent of her lost weight and seemed to recover fully.

The eggs appeared white with a surface texture not unlike the Parson's skin, each weighing slightly less than 0.1 ounce (2 grams). I divided them into three groups and placed them in Tupperware containers, the lids of which had approximately a dozen pinhole-size perforations. The substrate used in the containers was varied to ascertain whether the eggs would develop differently in different media. Two containers had a mixture of 80 percent vermiculite and 20 percent sterile soil; the third container had 80 percent sterile soil and 20 percent vermiculite.

The question of how to properly incubate the eggs required some thought. Realizing that the adults are exposed to a wide range of temperatures and a dormant period, it was a fair assumption that the eggs would diapause (remain at this stage for a certain amount of time), and the length of incubation had not been determined. Drawing from the limited information available and communications with colleagues, I decided to incubate the eggs for the first three months at approximately 74°F (23°C). The next three months, the eggs would be subjected to a temperature of 65°F

The author has had varying success in incubating Parson's chameleon eggs.

(18°C). After that, the temperature would be slowly increased to 74°F (23°C) over several weeks.

During the first three months, the development of the eggs was nominal. Five of the eggs became moldy; upon opening them I found no indications of fertility (these were the eggs found in the outside cage). In the process of opening the eggs, I discovered that the shell thickness of the egg was almost twice that of *Chamaeleo* species' eggs. In mid-December, another egg molded and showed no signs of development. As the incubation continued, the eggs were candled for signs of vascularization (having abnormal or an excessive number of blood vessels) and appeared clear yellow. I realized, however, that candling would be somewhat limited because of the shell thickness. Over the next six months, the remaining eggs increased in size by 10 percent. The egg development between the two substrates showed no significant difference. The eggs were candled once a month, and while there was no clear indication of vascularization, there was a change in the color in the seventh month to a reddish orange. The temperature was maintained primarily at 74°F (23°C), and although the eggs were exposed to higher temperatures throughout the summer, they never exceeded 80°F (26.7°C). At the one-year mark, the egg size had increased by 20 percent. Candling indicated further embryonic development, but again, due to shell thickness, it was unclear as to how far the development had progressed.

In October, well over a year after the eggs were laid, one egg showed a wet appearance. After several days, the egg began to shrink and discolor. I opened the egg and found inside a solid yolk and an embryo approximately 1/8-inch long within the yolk mass. Over the next four months, three more eggs repeated the same sequence, but inside the eggs were embryos of increasing size. The embryonic development was in the later stages, the largest embryo being close to 1½ in.

The eggs were put through a second cool-down period of three months from November through January at the same temperature as the first cool-down. Although all the substrate had been kept at the same level of moisture, the eggs in the container with the higher soil content started to develop differently. As the eggs began to increase in size, they developed what appeared to be stretch marks, the outer layer of the eggshell separating in irregular splits. The eggs in the other containers did not show this development. I wondered if this splitting acted as a means of reducing the thickness of the eggshell to facilitate the embryo's emergence. In April, the eggs were into the twenty-first month of incubation. On April 25, one egg had a single slit but was not preceded by signs of typical sweating. By the 26th, there were two more slits but no further development. On April 29, I opened the egg and inside was a fully formed neonate. It was alive but showed no signs of movement except for the tail when it was touched; this neonate died five days later. On the 29th, another egg was found with a single slit, and again there was no further development. On June 1, this egg was opened and another fully formed neonate was found, but it was not living.

The eggs were checked for signs of hatching on the evening of June 4 and none was found. On the morning of the 5th, a third egg had seven slits in a starburst pattern at the end, and by 4 p.m. the neonate had emerged. The neonate weighed 0.08 ounce (2.3 grams) and was 3 ¼ in (8.3 cm) in total length. Its coloration was an overall brown with a cream stripe running down the ridge of the dorsum. The neonate was placed into a well-planted fine-screen cage.

In the last few weeks of the month, most of the remaining eggs continued to go through a disappointing and repeating pattern. The eggs would slit once with no further activity, or they would reduce in size and start to discolor. Examination of the eggs showed fully developed embryos, although none were living. The zigzag stretch mark patterns on some of the eggs may have been caused by excessive moisture. Two of these eggs appeared to have ruptured, both containing fully formed neonates.

On July 5, twenty-three months from oviposition, a second hatchling emerged. This neonate was significant in that it showed the typical white spot on each flank; otherwise it was identical to the first. None of the remaining few eggs hatched; upon opening these eggs, full-term, I found dead neonates.

I raised the two offspring in screen cages, and their husbandry was typical as with other baby chameleons. The growth of the two neonates was remarkable. They shed at three months of age and doubled their weight in the first two months. At six months, they weighed 0.58 and 0.71 ounces (16.5 and 20 grams), with a total length of 7 in and 9 in (18 cm and 23 cm), respectively. At seven months, the larger of the two appeared to show the emergence of a rostral process, indicating that it was a male. At the one-year mark, they were clearly a male and a female. The male's coloration began to show the initial signs of the adult turquoise blue with orange eye turrets. The female was an overall green in color.

The low hatch rate of this clutch was as perplexing as it was unfortunate, yet this has often been experienced with other montane *Chamaeleo* species. Research by Dr. Larry Talent (pers. comm.) suggests that dietary and vitamin A deficiency may result in a weakening of the neonates, preventing successful emergence. The areas of incubation temperature ranges and the dietary requirements of adult Parson's certainly need further exploration.

The original adult pair of *C. p. parsonii* continued to do well, going through a second dormant phase the following winter. Breeding behavior was observed again in the spring, and the following September the female pro-

A baby *C. p. parsonii* clasps a branch with its feet and tail.

duced a second clutch of forty eggs. The second clutch was incubated in 100 percent vermiculite substrate and went through a similar incubation. The results of second clutch incubation resulted in two successful hatchings, with their emergence at twenty-three and twenty-four months. Yet the rate of successful hatching showed no improvement. Another unrelated clutch from the second pair of *C. p. parsonii* was incubated at an overall moderate temperature with an average temperate of 72°F (22°C). The eggs were placed in the same type of containers in vermiculite and kept with the same water ratio as with other *Chamaeleo* species. The hatch rate with this clutch was more than 85 percent. Unfortunately, the female of my first pair died during egg laying on her third attempt.

Over the following years, several other clutches were produced by other pairs of *C. p. parsonii* in my care, and the success rate with these was also more than 85 percent. The added joy of hatching out a clutch of *C. p. cristifer* was also accomplished, with a hatching success rate of more than 85 percent. The average length of time for incubation with these groups of eggs was fourteen to sixteen months. This is a significantly shorter incubation time than the original twenty-four months. Overall, this is a considerable improvement in the hatching rate and incubation time. The offspring from these clutches have grown and come into maturity between three and four years of age.

Parson's chameleons such as this female are fascinating animals. Their captive breeding should be pursued vigorously.

With the improved hatching success came many questions as to what I had done differently. There are two significant factors to which I have attributed my success. The first and foremost is that I have the luxury of living in Southern California. This allows me to house my Parson's chameleons outside year-round. The benefits of the natural seasonal changes combined with natural sunlight permits them to go through seasonal variances similar to those in Madagascar. The second is that I have used a varied vitamin-mineral supplementation. I found that no one product was sufficient to reproduce the missing nutrients in any *Chamaeleo* spp. natural wild diet. I use a rotating supplementation routine, switching out Repti-Cal, Reptivite, Miner-All, Calcium carbonate, and Walkabout Farms Shade formula.

Once a month, I add a few drops of water-soluble liquid bird vitamins to the drinking water. The dry supplementation is dusted on the insect food prey twice a week in rotation. I also added pinky mice to the diet. One pinky was offered to each chameleon once or twice a month in the spring and summer months when the reptiles were most active. The incubation temperatures for the eggs were kept in the low 70s F (21°C–23°C) throughout incubation. The goal of trying to reproduce the natural environment and diet is certainly important and directly relates to successful reproduction in captivity.

Since the original publication of this book in 1995, several other keepers have found success in reproduction of Parson's chameleons. Keepers in Germany, Italy, England, and the United States have had varied results in hatching success. The captive reproductive success with *C. p. parsonii* has improved and has even produced an F2 generation! Considering that I was told that my original pair would never survive in captivity, I am very pleased at my success in maintaining and propagating this fascinating species. Don't be afraid to try something that no one has done before: it can be done.

Conclusion

Much has been discovered about the captive care of *C. p. parsonii.* I hope I have provided some basic aspects of the captive care, reproduction, incubation, and hatching of *C. p. parsonii.* This information will help to further the overall understanding of the complexities for the reproduction of all chameleon species in captivity.

Because of their rarity, prohibitive cost, size, and large cage requirements, the Parson's chameleon may not be an ideal choice for everyone. However, these gentle giants are well worth the effort to continue further research into their husbandry. While their reproduction has been improved, it is still a random and far from regular event. The overall captive breeding success does not outweigh the loss of these creatures in both their native lands due to population encroachment on their habitat and the high losses sustained in poorly maintained captive situations. These magnificent reptiles are true jewels of nature. All care must be taken to preserve their ongoing existence on our planet.

REFERENCES

Albignec, R., A. Jolly, and P. Oberle. 1984. *Key environments: Madagascar*. Pergamon Press.

Allen, M. E., and O. T. Oftedal. 1989. Dietary manipulation of the calcium content of feed crickets. *Journal of Zoo and Wildlife Medicine* 20: 26–33.

Annis, J. A. 1992. Hypervitaminosis in chameleons: Are we unknowingly overdosing our animals on vitamin A? *Chameleon Information Network* 9: 18–25.

Atsatt, S. R. 1953. Storage of sperm in the female chameleon *Microsaura pumila pumila. Copeia* 1953(1): 59.

Bartlett, R. D, and P. Bartlett. 2001. *Jackson's and veiled chameleons (Reptile Keeper's Guides)*. Barron's Educational Series.

Bishop, C. A., and K. E. Pettit. 1992. Declines in Canadian amphibian populations: Designing a national monitoring strategy. Canadian Wildlife Services Occasional Paper, no. 76: 1–120.

Blanc, F. 1974. Table de développement de *Chamaeleo lateralis* Gray, 1831. *Annales d'Embryologie et de Morphogenèse* 7: 99–115.

Boulenger, G. A. 1896. Description of a new chameleon from Uganda. *Annals and Magazine of Natural History*, ser. 6, 17: 376.

Bourgat, R. 1970. Recherches écologiques et biologiques sur le *Chamaeleo pardalis* Cuvier 1829 de l'Isle de la Réunion et de Madagascar. *Bulletin de la Société Zoologique de France* 95: 259–268.

Brock, R. 1992. A chameleon with a party hat. *Zoonews*. San Diego Zoological Society: 6–8.

Brygoo, E. R. 1971a. Reptiliens Sauriens Chamaeleonidae. Genre *Chamaeleo. Faune de Madagascar* 33: 1–138.

———. 1971b. Reptiles *Sauriens Chamaeleonidae*: Genre *Chamaeleo. Faune de Madagascar* (Paris: Orston et CNRS) 33: 223–40.

Buckley, R. 1990. Experiments with habitat trees: Notes on the captive management of chameleons. *The Vivarium* 3(3): 10–29.

———. 1991. Experiments with habitat trees. *The Vivarium* 3(3): 10–30.

Bustard, H. R. 1958. Use of horns by *Chamaeleo jacksonii. British Journal of Herpetology* 2: 105–107.

Carpenter, A. I., O. Robson, J. M. Rowcliffe, and A. R. Watkinson. 2005. The impacts of international and national governance changes on a traded resource: A case study of Madagascar and its chameleon trade. *Biological Conservation* 123: 279–287.

Carpenter, A. I., J. M. Rowcliffe, and A. R. Watkinson. 2004. The dynamics of the global trade in chameleons. *Biological Conservation* 120: 291–301.

Castle, E. 1990. Captive reproduction and neonate husbandry of the oustalet's chameleon, *Cal. oustaleti*, at the Oklahoma City Zoological Park. Fourteenth International Herpetological Symposium on Captive Propagation and Husbandry, 25–34.

De Vosjoli, P. 1990a. *The general care and maintenance of true chameleons. Part 1: Husbandry*. Lakeside, Calif: Advanced Vivarium Systems.

———. 1990b. *The general care and maintenance of the true*

chameleons. Part II: Notes of popular species, disease and disorders. Lakeside, Calif: Advanced Vivarium Systems.
———. 1994. *The lizard keeper's handbook.* Lakeside, Calif: Advanced Vivarium Systems.

DeWitt, C. 1988. Jackson's chameleons, *Chamaeleo jacksonii*: Captive behavior, care, and breeding. *The Vivarium* 1(2): 17–20.

Eason, P. 1990. The effect of recent diet on prey choice in Senegalese chameleons (*Chamaeleo senegalensis*). *Journal of Herpetology* 24(4): 383–387.

Eason, P., G. W. Ferguson, and J. Hebrard. 1988. Variation in *Chamaeleo jacksonii* (Sauria, Chamaeleontidae): Description of a new subspecies. *Copeia* 1988(3): 580–590.

Esselte Map Service and Lidman Production AB. 1986. *Sweden: Graphic Learning Earth Book World Atlas.*

Ferguson, G. W. 1991. Ad-libitum feeding rates, growth, and survival of captive-hatched chameleons (*Chamaeleo pardalis*) from Nosy Bé Island, Madagascar. *Herpetological Review* 22: 124–125.
———. 1994. Old World chameleons in captivity: Growth, maturity, and reproduction of Malagasy panther chameleons (*Chamaeleo pardalis*). In *captive management and conservation of amphibians and reptiles*, edited by J. B. Murphy, K. Adler, and J. T. Collins, Society for the Study of Reptiles and Amphibians. *Contributions to Herpetology*, vol. 11.

Ferguson, G. W., W. H. Gehrmann, T. C. Chen, E. S. Dierenfeld, M. F. Holick. 2002. Effects of artificial ultraviolet light exposure on reproductive success of the female panther chameleon (*Furcifer pardalis*). *Zoo Biology* 21: 525–537.

Ferguson, G. W., W. H. Gehrmann, T. C. Chen, and M. F. Holick. 2005. Vitamin D content of the eggs of the panther chameleon *Furcifer pardalis*: Its relationship to UVB exposure/vitamin D-condition of the mother, incubation, and hatching success. *Journal of Herpetological Medicine and Surgery* 15: 9–13.

Ferguson, G. W., W. H. Gehrmann, K. B. Karsten, S. H. Hammack, M. McRae, T. C. Chen , N. P. Lung, and M. F. Holick. 2003. Do panther chameleons bask to regulate endogenous vitamin D3 production? *Physiological and Biochemical Zoology* 76: 52–59.

Ferguson, G. W., J. R. Jones, W. H. Gehrmann, S. H. Hammack, L. G. Talent, R. D. Hudson, E. S. Dierenfeld, M. P. Fitzpatrick, F. L. Frye, M. F. Holick, T. C. Chen, Z. Lu, T. S. Gross, and J. J. Vogel. 1996. Indoor husbandry of the panther chameleon *Chamaeleo (Furcifer) pardalis*: Effects of dietary vitamins A and D and ultraviolet irradiation on pathology and life-history traits. *Zoo Biology* 15: 279–299.

Ferguson, G. W., J. B. Murphy, and R. Hudson. 1990. The quest for the Mount Kenya Muriyu. *The Vivarium* 3(1): 18–38.

Ferguson, G. W., J. B. Murphy, A. Raselimanana, and J. B. Ramanamanjato. 2004. *The Panther chameleon: Color variation, natural history, conservation, and captive management*. Malabar, Fla: Krieger.

Frigg, M., and J. Broz. 1984. Relationships between vitamin A and vitamin E in the chick. *International Journal for Vitamin and Nutrition Research* 54: 125–134.

Fritz, J., and F. Schutte. 1987. The biology of the Yemen *C. calyptratus*, Durmeril and Durmeril (1981): With remarks on its systematic status (Sauria: Chamaeleonidae). *Salamandra* 23(1): 17–25.

Frye, F. L. 1991. *Biomedical and surgical aspects of captive reptile husbandry*. 2nd ed. Vol. 1. Malabar, Fla: Krieger, 488.

Gehrmann W. H., J. D. Horner, G. W. Ferguson, T. C. Chen, and M. F. Holick. 2004. A comparison of responses by three broadband radiometers to different ultraviolet-B sources. *Zoo Biology* 23: 355–363.

Glaw, F., and M. Vences. 1993. *A field guide to the amphibians and reptiles of Madagascar*. Privately published.

———. 1994. *A field guide to the amphibians and reptiles of Madagascar*. 2nd ed. Koln, Germany: Moos Druck, Leverkusen and FARBO, 231–257.

Henkel, F. W., and S. Heinecke. 1993. *Chameleons in terrarium.* Hannover: Landbuch Verlag.

Hillenius, D. 1959. The differentiation within the genus *Chamaeleo* Laurenti 1768. *Beaufortia* 8 (89): 1–92.

———. 1966. Notes on chameleons III: The chameleons of Southern Arabia. *Beaufortia* 13(156): 91–108.

Hillenius, D., and Gasperetti, J. 1984. The reptiles of Saudi Arabia, the chameleons of Saudi Arabia. *Fauna of Saudi Arabia* 6: 513–526.

Holick M. F. 2004. Vitamin D: Importance in the prevention of cancers, type 1 diabetes, heart disease, and osteoporosis. *American Journal of Clinical Nutrition*. 79: 362–371.

Houghton, R. A., and G. M. Woodwell. 1989. Global climatic change. *Scientific American*. 260: 36–44.

Jenkins, J. R. 1992. Husbandry and diseases of Old World chameleons. *Journal of Small Exotic Animal Medicine* 1(4): 166–171.

Landwer, A. J. 1994. Manipulation of egg production reveals cost of reproduction in the tree lizard (*Urosaurus ornatus*). *Oecologia* 100: 243–249.

McKeown, S. 1978. *Hawaiian reptiles and amphibians.* Honolulu: Oriental, 32–33.

———. 1991. Jackson's chameleons in Hawaii are the recently described Mt. Kenya subspecies, *Chamaeleo jacksonii xantholophus.* Bulletin of Chicago Herpetological Society 26(3): 49.

McKeown, S. 1991. Second-generation panther chameleons bred at the Chaffee Zoo. *American Association of Zoological Parks and Aquariums Communique* August: 14.

Modry, D., and B. Koudela. 1998. Veiled chameleons: Isosporan infections of *Chamaeleo calyptratus* representing problems for its breeding in captivity. *Reptile and Amphibian Magazine* 54: 38–41.

Necas, P. 1991. *Chamaeleo calyptratus calyptratus. Herpetofauna*, 13 (73): 6–9.

———. 2004. *Chameleons, Nature's Hidden Jewels.* 2nd ed. Frankfurt am Main, Germany: Edition Chimaira, 113–119.

Parcher, S. R. 1974. Observations on the natural histories of six Malagasy chamaeleontidae. *Zeitschrift für Tierpsychologie* 34: 500–523.

Preston-Mafham, K. 1991. *Madagascar: A natural history.* New York, NY: Facts on File.

Rand, A. S. 1958. A new subspecies of *Chamaeleo jacksonii* Boulenger, and a key to the species of three-horned chameleons. *Breviora* (Museum of Comparative Zoology, Harvard) 99: 1–8.

———. 1961. A suggested function of the ornamentation of East African forest chameleons. *Copeia* 1961(4): 411–414.

Raxworthy, C. J. 1988. Reptiles, rain forest, and conservation in Madagascar. *Biological Conservation* 43: 181–211.

Schmidt, W. K., K. Tamm, and E. Wallikewitz. 1989. *Chameleons: Drachen unserer Zeit.* Munster: Herpetologischer Fachverlag.

Schneider, S. H. 1989. The changing climate. *Scientific American* 261: 70–79.

Stahl, S. J., and C. J. Blackburn. 1996. Captive husbandry and reproduction of the veiled chameleon, *Chamaeleo calyptratus. The Vivarium* 8(1): 28–31.

Tornier, J. 1903. Drei neue Reptilien aus Ost-Afrika. *Zoologische Jahrbücher, Abtheilung für Systematik, Geographie und Biologie der Tiere* 19:173–178.

Zug, G. R. 1993. *Herpetology: An introductory biology of amphibians and reptiles.* San Diego: Academic Press, 413–415.

INDEX

S

T

U

V

W

Y

ABOUT THE AUTHORS

Gary Ferguson

Gary Ferguson was born in Cheyenne, Wyoming, in 1941 but spent most of his youth in Virginia. He began keeping herps at the age of nine; however, despite a boyhood fascination with old-world chameleons had to wait until the age of thirty-six before obtaining his first one. Gary has three degrees, a BS from Tulane University, an MS from Texas Tech University, and a PhD from the University of Michigan. Currently a professor at Texas Christian University, he is widely known for his scientific publications in the fields of behavior, ecology, evolution, and nutrition of lizards.

Kenneth Kalisch

Kenneth Kalisch began keeping chameleons in the mid 1980s; his interest grew to encompass the care of more than thirty different species of *Chamaeleo*, *Calumma*, *Furcifer*, *Bradypodion*, *Brookesia*, and *Rhampholeon*. He has successfully reproduced more than twenty species and was one of the first to breed and hatch *Calumma parsonii parsonii* and *Calumma parsonii cristifer* in captivity. He was one of the founding editors of *CHAMELEONS!*, an online e-magazine working toward furthering knowledge about these amazing reptiles. He is a past editor of *The Chameleon Information Network.*

Sean McKeown, 1944–2002

Sean McKeown was a well-known herpetologist in the United States. He held supervising herpetologist and curator of reptiles and amphibians in different zoos for over 20 years. He was the published author of *The General Care and Maintenance of Day Geckos* and *A Field Guide to Reptiles in the Hawaiian Islands.*